# From Soupy To Nuts!

## A HISTORY OF DETROIT TELEVISION

## by Tim Kiska

*Momentum Books LLC*
*Royal Oak, Michigan*

Published by Momentum Books, L.L.C.

117 West Third St
Royal Oak, MI 48067
www.momentumbooks.com

Printed and bound in the U.S.A.

ISBN-13: 978-1-879094-70-3
ISBN-10: 1-879094-70-3
LCCN: 2005921502

*To my wife, Patricia, and my children, Caitlin, Amy and Eric.*

# Table of Contents

# *Foreword*

# *By Sonny Eliot*

If you were to ask me what kind of writing is the most profitable, the answer would be easy: ransom notes. If you were to ask what kind of writing pays the least, the answer would also be easy: prologues, introductions and love notes. And so this prologue, introduction and love note is being paid for in something better than money. Plain, old-fashioned pleasure. My pleasure.

Timothy Kiska is not only a friend, he's a helluva fine writer and a respected former television critic for *The Detroit News*. Nonetheless, Timothy, showing an amazing lack of judgment, asked me to compose a little something on TV in Detroit. Since I'd been in the eye of the iconoscope when it all began in Motown, way back when we were young, passionate and skinny, I nodded, smiled, and hid myself away to a secret place over the Lindell saloon to think, and to string a few phrases together. Ah, that clever Kiska. He appealed to my ego, of course. And who doesn't like having his ego massaged, amongst other things.

When old WWJ-TV, Channel 4, fired up that mysterious maze of wires and electronic doo-dads back in March of 1947, it became the very first TV station in Michigan and, for the next 18 months, had no competition. The first sponsor was the late, great original J.L. Hudson's Department Store, and the first studio was a marvelous radio studio, converted and outfitted to be a new TV studio. The client's booth became the engineer's control room, the cameras were giant-eyed "DuMont-Tanks" with one large lens and a 1-foot square transformer attached to the camera by a thick cable. It was on the floor next to the camera and dragged along whenever the camera moved, which wasn't too often. The lights were hot—hotter than a fireman's destination. The plastic tile floor just curled up and died and had to be replaced immediately. If you were "on-camera" for as little as 10 minutes, those 800-1,000 foot-candle overheads guaranteed not only bright red skin, but also little wisps of steam rising from every pore. You could certainly part your hair in the middle and irrigate your eyebrows.

In the early days, it was hard to believe that Channel 4 televised 118 hours of *live* television per week: Everything from beauty contests, sewing demonstrations, midget auto racing, wrestling (of course), boxing, cooking shows and, as required by the Federal Communications Commission, the throw-away, not-profitable news shows—shows that presumably separated the wheat from the chaff and the chicken from the gumbo.

Way back in the 1940s, when TV was still a gleam in David Sarnoff's eye, the coaxial cable from the East Coast hadn't yet reached as far west as Detroit. Premier station WWJ-TV was owned and operated (at a considerable profit) by that wondrous newspaper, *The Detroit News,* which was owned and operated by the Evening News Association (also at a considerable profit). Channel 4 began tentatively to grow in both competence and importance. Back then we didn't reckon with TV's great influence, and hardly realized how it would change our lives. It was just something new, exciting and experimental. You learned on the job.

There wasn't much film in the late '40s, and videotape was still an investor's dream. Newspaper pictures were used, focused and flipped. Pictures were borrowed from the *News* and *Free Press,* reluctantly loaned. After all, they were being lent to a presumed competitor. During those first few years, I don't think anyone realized that the giant eye in a box, sitting in the front room, would have an impact so great that the world would never be the same again. Art was being changed by technology and technology was being changed by art. The technology of today is staggering and sensational—oftentimes unbelievable. Yesteryear's TV and today is like comparing mud to ice cream.

By 1949, every appliance store in Michigan had sold out of TV sets—even the big 10-inch ones. Milton Berle and his show burned hotter and brighter than anything, anywhere on, in or out of show business. Television was exciting, controversial and here to stay, an invention that was surprising, delightful and unbelievable. No one knew how it worked. But it worked.

Ah well, back to the libretto—so many shows, so many actors, actresses, announcers, producers and performers run through my memory bank, so many half-remembered moments from everyone's past, such a wealth of nostalgia, long and loving, of TV in Detroit, spring back into focus just thumbing through the pages of this book. It's like a stroll through a familiar neighborhood to visit old and new friends—friends whose names you may remember, if you're old enough, or people and shows that have no meaning at all, but are interesting to read about. Names like Paul Williams, Fran Harris, Walt Koste, Pat Tobin, Johnny Slagle, Bob Maxwell, Minnie Jo Curtis, Dick Osgood, Willy Dooit, Seymour Kapetansky, Dick Westerkamp, Don Kremer and Rube Weiss. The list goes on and on and on—and time, the stuff of which life is made, goes right along with it. Enjoy Timothy's book. It's a fine little snapshot of TV life you'll enjoy.

# Author's Introduction

This is a celebration of Detroit television, when TV was as local as Vernors, Sanders Hot Fudge and Hudson's.

There was room for clowns, bowlers, baseball players, philosophers, journalists, adventurers, movie mavens, wrestlers, comedians, commentators, cooks and magicians. The people who put these shows on the air ran the gamut, too. There were drunks, geniuses, thugs, heroes, artists, craftsmen, hustlers and poets. Some of the people in this book were all of these things at times. A few were all these things before lunch.

In the early days, nobody knew if the new medium would make money, so the people who worked in it had no worries about the profit imperative. That gave them freedom to perform or write as they wished.

And it contributed to Detroit's sense of community. A Cub Scout troop could visit "The Sagebrush Shorty Show," or youngsters could watch their classmates do the limbo with Poopdeck Paul.

Go from city to city now, and local television looks the same. Every city has Oprah and whatever shock talk is selling. Even local news looks the same, regardless of locale. It is as if a biochemical laboratory somewhere produces on-air talent—attractive, congenial, with a professional veneer, but, somehow, not very real.

What has happened to television is the same thing that has happened to food. Long ago, ordinary food in Louisville wasn't the same as ordinary food in Detroit or New Orleans. Now, like food, the TV franchise tastes the same everywhere. At the start of the new millennium, a 12-year-old wrestling fan in Los Angeles sees The Rock the same as a 12-year-old wrestling fan in Detroit. But in the 1960s, a 12-year-old in Detroit watched Lord Layton. In 1960s Los Angeles, nobody had any idea who Lord Layton might be.

With the evaporation of distinctive local television, a piece of our local character disappeared. Bob Seger and many Motown acts received their first big exposure in the 1960s on local dance shows such as Channel 9's *Swingin' Time* and Channel 7's *Club 1270*. It was local television that introduced Detroit teens to these artists. Fast forward to the late 1990s when a young musical artist from Romeo by the name of Kid Rock broke into the big time via television. Detroit teens, just like teens in L.A., saw him on MTV. There simply was no place on local television for a guy like Kid Rock to take wing.

And when somebody decided that 36th District Court Judge Greg Mathis had talent as a television judge, that somebody wasn't anybody in Detroit television. It was a Los Angeles-based syndication company. Years ago, Judge Mathis probably would have appeared on a Detroit version of *Traffic Court*.

Is television better as a result? Or is it merely national? Thousands of Detroiters traveled to the Channel 4 studio to see *Milky the Clown*, or to Channel 9 to dance on *Swingin' Time*, or to Channel 62 to dance on *The Scene*. Today, if you want to see Oprah Winfrey in the flesh, you've got to drive to Chicago. And even then, good luck. Getting a ticket to *Oprah* is about as easy as getting a ticket to see the Pope celebrate Easter Mass.

Television programs, particularly daytime television, have certainly become a whole lot less wholesome. Witness these program listings for May 1, 2000: Jenny Jones did a program on "promiscuous" teens; Maury Povich waxed eloquent on "oversexed" teens; Montel Williams focused on "out-of-control" teens. Does anybody see a pattern here? The mission of George Pierrot, Bill Kennedy and Rita Bell was to entertain and educate. For Maury, Montel and Jenny, Job One is to shock.

Nobody is to blame, really. Television is a business. If somebody tried to put George Pierrot and his travel movies on the air today, few would watch. The local TV station that did that would have to pay Pierrot (or somebody like him), stagehands, camera operators and more than a few producers. And then? The viewer interested in checking out travel could watch cable television's Travel Channel. Teenage rock 'n' rollers can catch up with the latest news and trends on MTV. Who could compete on a local level?

It's all very sad. The demolition of the downtown Hudson's building was a major event—as it should be. It marked a passing. The same thing happened to local television—except it wasn't quite as dramatic. There was no final scene. The local medium was gradually dismantled, brick by brick. George Pierrot retired. Sonny Eliot was canned. *Bowling For Dollars* went away, and that was probably the death knell. Channel 62, before it was bought by CBS, continued on with an interesting selection of local video. Marilyn Turner's show was cancelled in 1995, the last of the only non-news daily programs on TV.

It's now a hard business, its content determined not by creative instinct but by market surveys, focus groups and state-of-the-art ratings services. But the soft part of it—the creativity, the warmth, the heart, the improbable and programming that kept the test patterns from bumping into each other—still lives on in the memories of those who saw it.

Tim Kiska
February 2005

# Kids

*Soupy, Milky and Sagebrush Shorty.*
*These, among others, were the video babysitters*
*to a generation of Detroiters.*

### Adler, Clyde (d: 1993)

He was local television's greatest unseen force during the 1950s. It was Adler who gave life and voice to the most popular characters on *Lunch With Soupy*—White Fang and Black Tooth. White Fang was the "meanest dog in all of Deetroit" and Black Tooth was his antithesis—"the sweetest dog in all of Deetroit." Rounding out the cast was Pookie, a chipper, pint-sized lion who whistled, and Hippy the Hippo, who never spoke. The creation of these amazing characters was a random act of artistry. "It was by happenstance—a fluke," recalls Jane Adler, Clyde's widow. "He and Soupy were discussing the show one day and Clyde said to Soupy, 'If we just had a dog … and a sound." Later, Jane Adler recalled her husband telling her: "That sound … don't tell anybody what I do for a living—growling like an animal. They'll think you're crazy."

Clyde Adler, the brains (and hands) behind White Fang and Black Tooth.

**The Romper Room mantra, at the end of each show:**

Romper, bomper,
stomper, boo.
Tell me, tell me,
tell me, do.
Have all the children
been good today?
And put all their toys away?
I see ...

Adler grew up in Grosse Pointe, a graduate of the Grosse Pointe High School class of 1944. As a student, he kept himself busy with work in local community theatre groups and played clarinet in the Pierce Middle School band. After U.S. Navy service during World War II and graduation from Michigan State University, Adler went to work at Channel 7 as a stage manager and a director. It was while working as a director that he created White Fang and the rest of the characters, so he signed on with Sales full-time.

White Fang and Black Tooth made Adler one of local TV's biggest stars, although viewers never saw his face. The closest thing they saw was his hands. He was the guy who'd knock on Soupy's door. Other than that, Adler was virtually anonymous. When Sales took his show to California in 1960, Adler went along. He took a cut in pay to do so, but the show was almost as big in Los Angeles as it had been in Detroit. Angelinos even formed their own Clyde Adler Fan Club during the 1960s.

But after roughly a decade of giving life to this entertaining animal menagerie, Adler opted out. Sales moved to New York City, the country's biggest broadcast market, but Adler stayed behind in California. An insulin-dependent diabetic, Adler complained about the difficulty of keeping up with the physical demands of the show. So he stayed behind doing technical chores for ABC's Los Angeles television station. Among Adler's jobs: working on the lighting crew for *The Lawrence Welk Show*. Jim Henson, creator of *The Muppets*, tried to hire Adler. Adler politely declined the invitation.

Family demands brought Adler and his wife back to Detroit in 1971, and Adler returned to Channel 7—initially as a temporary employee. He quietly sat out the rest of his career happily working the technical end of operations at Channel 7. Some performers require applause the way most people require air. Fame never mattered to Adler. He rarely mentioned his enormous contribution to colleagues unless they brought it up first. When historian Richard Bak wrote a history of children's TV several years ago, Adler declined a taped interview. "There was not a conceited bone in his body," said Jane Adler. Adler retired from Channel 7 in 1989. He died four years later.

## Ardis, Miss

Most big cities had a local version of *Romper Room*. A Baltimore company, Claster Productions, dreamed up the concept and sold the franchise to broadcasters throughout the country. Ardis Kenealy hosted Detroit's version, which aired on Channel 4 throughout the 1950s. The Detroit native and Wayne State University grad worked as a model before morphing into Miss Ardis. She is now retired and lives in Bingham Farms.

## Bozo the Clown

Most major cities in the United States had a Bozo the Clown in the 1960s and 1970s. Detroit's Bozos (um … Bozi?) were Robert "Bob" McNea and Art Cervi.

Alan W. Livingston originally created "Bozo" in 1946 for Capitol Records, which had interest in producing a children's "read along" record. (Larry Harmon Productions later purchased the Bozo license from Capitol in the late 1950s.) Livingston was said to have portrayed the first TV Bozo in southern California some three years later. After that, the red wig and bulbous nose became a franchise, and Bozo spread from television station to television station. (Willard Scott once played a television Bozo in Washington, D.C.)

Channel 4 bought the Bozo franchise for Detroit, and settled on Bob McNea to do the job. McNea, a Canadian who had experience playing a clown, had also worked as a character actor on Detroit television. At one point, McNea was doing nine hours of live television weekly—one hour daily on weekdays 4-5 p.m., plus two hours daily on weekends. He played the part from 1959

Art Cervi, the ultimate Bozo.

## The Faygo Kid to the Rescue

(spoken)
Which way did he go? Which way did he go?
He went for FAYGO!

(sung)
Oh, the stagecoach was a headin' through the mountain.
The stage, they called the Wells Faygo Express.
The cargo, so I hear
Faygo Old-Fashioned Root Beer.
The tasty drink with creamy head goodness.

(spoken)
Lookout!
It's a holdup!
It's Black Bart!

(female voice)
Oh, save me!
For my life I fear!

(Bart)
Oh, hush up, gal.
It's that famous drink I want.
That case of famous Old-Fashioned Root Beer!

(Faygo Kid)
Stand where you are.
Black Bart, you are through.

(Bart)
It's the Faygo kid!

(Faygo Kid)
Madame, do not fear!
I will save your Faygo Old-Fashioned Root Beer!

(Gun Shots — shave and a haircut — click click; bass drum sound)

*Continued on pg. 9*

until 1967, when Channel 4 lost the Bozo franchise to Channel 9. At that point, McNea morphed into Oopsy! the Clown.

Channel 9 had some difficulties casting a new Bozo. While it may be easy to be *a* Bozo, it's not that easy being *the* Bozo. Jerry Booth, who played the Jingles character at Channel 9, tried it for a very short time and refused to do it any longer. Another Bozo lasted one day.

McNea's eventual permanent replacement at Channel 9 had the oddest career beginnings of anybody in this book. Art Cervi started out in the furniture business, managing the Pleasure and Leisure Shops, which had outposts in Redford and Garden City. When radio caught Cervi's attention, he pursued the program director at WOMC-FM until he was hired. Eventually, he worked his way up to become WKNR-AM's (Keener 13) music director, where Cervi and Robin Seymour struck up a friendship. From Keener 13, Cervi ended up across the river at Channel 9 booking talent and shepherding audiences into the station for live shows.

When Channel 9 acquired the Bozo license for Detroit from Larry Harmon Productions, the station held open auditions. Virtually everybody who wasn't too embarrassed to parade around in a red wig and red nose showed up. Hey, this was TV! At first, Cervi had no interest in trying out. "But they kept hounding me because I worked so well with the kids. They kept telling me it'd take maybe 15 minutes. So I put the suit on, cut a tape and forgot about it," he later recalled.

When Cervi was summoned to the boss's office at Channel 9, he wasn't certain what was up. "He was sitting in front of two stacks of tape, each about a foot high. And he told me, 'I don't know what we're going to do with you. You are, by far, the best of all the candidates. But you have the least on-camera experience. Let's try this for 30 days.'"

The Bozo gig—five days a week of live TV—lasted until 1975 on Channel 9, plus another five years on Channel 2 until 1980.

Detroiters might be disappointed to discover that an oft-repeated legend about an incident on the Bozo show never happened. The legend goes that a child, missing a shot with Bozo Bucks, begins swearing. The legend continues that Bozo says: "That's a Bozo No-No," to which the child replies—depending on the version—"Cram it, clown," "Ram it, clownie," or "F*ck off, clown." Says Cervi: "It never happened. But I'm still asked about it. Constantly." Baby Boomers in many other U.S. cities such as L.A. and Boston also claim it happened there, too.

## Booth, Jerry

Booth starred in a trio of 1960s-era Channel 9 kid's shows: *Jingles In Boofland*, *The Larry and Jerry Show*, and *Jerry Booth's Fun House*. He was at the station from 1958-1968, and was Bozo for three or four months. "It was more than I could handle," said Booth.

Booth went to Millikin University in Decatur, Illinois, majoring in—oddly enough—business administration and broadcasting. A college professor suggested Booth try radio. Booth took up the suggestion, catching the show-biz bug. Booth created the Jingles format in WPTA-TV in Fort Wayne, Indiana, in the late 1950s. Jingles dressed in a jester outfit and did his act in a set designed as a castle. The set might have been the cheesiest in Detroit TV, and looked as if it had been assembled from discarded refrigerator boxes. Jingles's sidekicks included Herkimer the Dragon, Cecil B. Rabbit—who was the "world's known authority on everything." Cecil B., of course, sounded a lot like Paul Harvey. On *Fun House*, Booth worked from what appeared to be a log cabin, where he joshed with Clyde the Moose. Clyde, whose full name was Clyde Casual, was particularly easy to write for: The only thing he ever said was "Uh-huh."

In addition to doing Jingles, Booth would do local theatre on occasion, taking a part in *Annie Get Your Gun* for the Avon

*Continued from pg. 8*

(sung)
So the stagecoach went on headin' through the mountains.
And old Black Bart went off to jail, I hear.

(Bart)
The Faygo kid.
Which way did he go?
Which way did he go?

He went for FAYGO!!!
(sung)
He went for Faygo Old-Fashioned Root Beer!

Jerry Booth, the czar of Boofland.

Miss Flora, a.k.a. Flora Asseltine.

Players in Rochester, Michigan. Such was his fame that he started a small amusement park in Windsor. It consisted of a mid-sized roller coaster, plywood cutouts of castles and a few bumper cars. It lasted a year. Since leaving television, Booth moved to California and works in sales.

## Flora, Miss

She hosted Channel 9's *Romper Room* from 1959 until 1967. When Channel 9 producers searched for a hostess for their new kiddie show during the late 1950s, they were looking for a woman in her early 20s, preferably a teacher. Flora (full name: Flora Asseltine) was 38 and had never taught a class. Her show business efforts were limited to work in Windsor's light opera troupe. But she understood children, since she had two of her own.

Her status as mother, along with her limitless and obvious charm, apparently earned her the job. "They handed me a glass of milk and asked me to make up my own commercial, right there on the spot. Well, I talked about milk, and broadened the topic to include cottage cheese, as well. I finally stopped and apologized, saying, 'Oh dear, I seem to have gotten far afield.'"

As Miss Flora, she entertained a generation of youngsters on both sides of the Detroit River. Viewers could never have guessed the tragedy that she experienced during the show: Her husband died on a Friday. Miss Flora buried him on a Monday. Station officials urged her to return to work on a Tuesday. She did, without uttering a word about her experience. "Nobody," she said years later, "ever knew."

She remarried, retired from television, and lives a peaceful life in Windsor.

## Ginger, Johnny

Johnny Ginger (real name: Gaylen Grindle) entertained youngsters on Channel 7 during the 1950s and most of the 1960s, inter-

Channel 7's Johnny Ginger.

lacing "Three Stooges" movies with his wacky form of physical humor. Sometimes he'd play an out-of-control bellhop; sometimes he'd lip-sync records.

A Toledo native and son of a vaudeville performer, Ginger was telling jokes in nightclubs when he was still a teenager. Even by then, he'd had plenty of experience, beginning a show-biz career with his vaudevillian parents at the age of 6. One of his early memories is of sitting on his father's lap, singing for a crowd. He was hired at Channel 7 in 1956, where he hosted *Curtain Time Theater*. "I was doing a show in Windsor when a guy named Pete Strand (Soupy Sales' producer) came in and asked if I'd like to do TV. My response was not a wise one. I said, 'What? Is Ed Sullivan moving on?'" Despite the wisecrack, Ginger impressed Channel 7 brass during an audition by falling off a stool.

Johnny Ginger and Sammy Davis Jr.

For a while, he had two shows on Channel 7—one at 8 a.m., the other at 6 p.m.—and also entertained at area supper clubs at night. And he appeared in a 1964 Three Stooges' movie, *The Outlaws Is Coming*, which was the trio's last film. (He remembers Moe Howard as a gentle soul.) All of this activity might explain the heart attack he suffered while still in his 20s. And there was a nervous breakdown somewhere in there. "I was working two shows a day and one on Saturday," he recalled later. "I had the heart attack and told the doctor, 'I don't believe this. I'm still young.' He told me, 'Your heart is only as good as you treat it.'"

Ginger left Channel 7 after about a decade and relocated to Channel 50, where he hosted another children's show. Sgt. Sacto eventually replaced Ginger. He returned home to Toledo during the late 1960s—but then hit the road again doing standup comedy. Ginger is on the road seven months per year. "I love it," he says, "and I still can't believe I get paid to do this."

The Hot Fudge gang.

## Hot Fudge

This was among the last locally produced children's shows on Detroit television. It debuted on Channel 7 in 1974 with Arte Johnson (*Laugh-In*) in the starring role. "We were more influenced by Sesame Street than other children's shows," recalls producer Barry Hurd, who ran the show during its second year with Bob Elnicky. "*Sesame Street* taught youngsters about reading and numbers. We wanted to teach them about emotion, teach them about themselves." To that end, the producers had a team of psychologists read the scripts.

Johnson left after the first year, and was replaced by a trio: Larry Santos (a well-known local singer who can still be heard on various ad jingles), actress Amanda Carruthers (who was later replaced by Yolanda Williams), and Ron Coden (a local folksinger-actor-comedian). Coden's characters included Professor Emotion, Detective Tomato, Mr. Nasty and Hiram Kneepad, giving the program comedic spark. *Hot Fudge* soon became hot stuff, and was syndicated nationwide. At its peak, it aired five days a week on some 90 stations throughout the country, including New York, Los Angeles, Chicago and San Francisco. It ceased production in 1980-81, continuing in reruns through 1985.

## Hunt, Bwana Don

Bwana Don's (real name: Don Hunt) jungle persona was no act. The Channel 2 star, who hosted a daily weekday morning show with pet chimp Bongo Bailey, was really into pets. And animals. And the African continent. Particularly the African continent. At one time or another he owned a Ferndale pet store and a 1,216-acre game preserve in Kenya, the Mt. Kenya Game Ranch, with the late William Holden. Hunt described himself as the "resident director, chief worker and irrepressible enthusiast" of the operation. It was there that Hunt saved a handful

Bwana Don: Out of Ferndale.

of animal species from extinction. One of those included the "Bongo," a forest antelope.

Hunt was a Ferndale native who worked his way through high school and three years of college (University of Detroit) at the pet store he later bought, and realized big money when the Parke-Davis & Co. drug firm ordered up a truckload of guinea pigs from Hunt's place. (It's assumed that Parke-Davis wasn't using the animals as pets.)

His Detroit TV career became the foundation for big things: a nationally syndicated show and a worldwide animal import business worth millions. In 1971, the *Wall Street Journal* profiled the Bwana Don empire. Bongo Bailey even got a mention.

After leaving television, Hunt moved permanently to Africa. He worked as an animal broker: giraffes were going for $5,000-$6,500, zebras from $2,000-$2,500.

Captain Jolly shows off "spinach power."

## Jolly, Captain (d: 1994)

Captain Jolly, played by entertainer Toby David, brought *Popeye* cartoons on Channel 9 to thousands of Baby Boomers. The Captain wore a sailor's cap tilted sideways, glasses, and a striped shirt, and introduced the cartoons in seafarer's lingo.

David was genetically pre-disposed to a life in entertainment. Both his parents worked in the circus—his father was a clarinet player, his mother an animal trainer. He was first heard on radio in 1935 doing voices for CKLW-AM's Ralph Binge and Joe Gentile, two of the most popular radio hosts of their day. During World War II, he worked as an entertainer in New York and Washington, D.C., and was noted for his effective campaign for the sale of war bonds.

David became Captain Jolly in 1957 on Channel 9, where he was seen weekdays at 6 p.m. "Poopdeck Paul" handled the weekend shifts. Captain Jolly was finally "beached" (in the words of *Detroit News* TV columnist Frank Judge) in 1964. He

Captain Jolly, a.k.a. Toby David.

13

Captain Jolly with fans.

**Can you believe it, shipmates? Captain Jolly busted Poopdeck Paul. The following is from Toby David's (Captain Jolly's) personal, unpublished memoirs.**

"As you will recall, Captain Jolly had a side-kick on the *Popeye Show* named Poopdeck Paul. In addition to appearing on my shows during the week, Paul hosted the weekend segments of the show. With the cancellation of the *Popeye* series, Paul (Paul Allen Schultz) found himself adrift. In a venture called Holiday Magic Cosmetics, one of those pyramid selling schemes that surfaced in the '60s, he made the mistake of using my name in his promotion and advertising materials. I got on the phone to the Attorney General of the State of Michigan as soon as I heard about it. This resulted in the hasty departure from the United States of Paul and his partner. I haven't the slightest idea where they are now.

"You never know, do you?"

later became "Captain Toby" for a brief time on Channel 7, but was out of television entirely by the mid-1960s. During his post-TV years, he worked for the State of Michigan, but eventually moved to Arizona, where he worked as a public relations official in the city of Scottsdale. He died at age 80 while performing for a group of senior citizens.

## Milky's Party Time (d: 1994)

This show made the phrase "Twin Pines" a permanent part of the Motor City lexicon. *Milky's Movie Party* debuted December 16, 1950, becoming a Baby Boomer favorite during the show's 17 years on Channels 2, 4 and 7. Throughout the 1950s, the program was broadcast live from Channel 4's studios in downtown Detroit for two hours on Saturday afternoons. Milky made personal appearances, as well. In his white clown outfit, conical hat, white makeup and dark eye shadow, Milky (as played by magician Clare Cummings) looked slightly surreal. Years after Cummings' death, the Detroit rap group Insane Clown Posse paid a backhanded tribute to the show by dressing up one of their characters in a Milky outfit. That made as much sense as placing Mr. Rogers among the Droogs in *A Clockwork Orange*, but the audience seemed to like it—even if they didn't quite get the joke.

What kids didn't know about Cummings was that he was a serious magician who had been a member of the International Brotherhood of Magicians since 1929. One would have to be a serious magician to keep kids entertained for nearly two decades. During the week, he worked as a paint salesman.

The show was pure, innocent entertainment, admirable in its simplicity. Kids would watch Milky do party tricks; or they might sing or dance, while their parents looked on from a glassed-in room out of the camera's view. Of course, a lucky kid would get to dip his or her hand into a jar of pennies.

Although Milky went off the air in 1967, Cummings continued performing until the age of 80.

## Oopsy! the Clown

After Channel 4 lost the Bozo franchise to Channel 9 in 1967, the station had to do something. Their solution? They put Bob McNea, who had played Bozo for eight years, into a different wig and suit and christened him "Oopsy! the Clown." To the station's

Milky, as played by Clare Cummings.

Cummings was also a serious magician.

Oopsy! the Clown, a.k.a. Bob McNea.

"Poopdeck Paul" Allen Schultz.

credit, Channel 4 never tried to deceive the audience. "You can't fool children," McNea later recalled. "I told our guys that there was no use denying it, people are going to know the guy who was playing Oopsy! played Bozo. We'd get these letters, often from children, saying, 'Hey, what gives?' So we'd write back, 'Bozo got a new suit and a haircut. Do you like it?'"

McNea liked playing Oopsy! better than Bozo. "That Bozo wig was awful," McNea recalls, "it was like having your head in a vise." *Oopsy!* lasted even longer than Bozo—it got the gate in 1979, not long after Post-Newsweek took ownership of Channel 4.

McNea—who was born in Canada, lived in Windsor, and remained a Canadian citizen throughout his 20 years playing a clown on Channel 4—took his wig and nose to Kitchener, Ontario, where he had a successful career. He maintained the legal rights to *Oopsy!* and syndicated the show across Canada.

## Poopdeck Paul (d: 2000)

Channel 9's Poopdeck Paul (real name: Paul Allen Schultz) hosted *Popeye* cartoons, mostly during the weekends, between 1956 and 1966. The cartoons, however, were a sideshow. The real attraction was Poopdeck Paul as master of ceremonies to various games and contests: When limbo, lip-syncing to Beatle records and miniature golf were all the rage, Poopdeck emceed contests. Schultz had a perfect pitch when it came to determining what interested youngsters. And he was a trailblazer in the way he presented it. While Captain Jolly stayed in the *Popeye* studio during the week, Schultz would hold the contests on the Channel 9 lawn.

It all ended abruptly. He was out in 1966. Within a few years, he hit the newspapers for his role in Holiday Magic Cosmetics, a business that Michigan's Attorney General judged to be a pyramid scheme. Schultz moved overseas for several decades before settling back in Ontario to care for his ill son. Schultz died in 2000.

## Ricky the Clown

Ricky the Clown (real name: Irv Romig) entertained Detroit youngsters between 1953 and 1965 on Channel 7. Although Ricky's bulbous red nose always remained, his program underwent several incarnations: *Tip-Top Fun* and *The Ricky the Clown Show* (1953-1956); the *Robin and Ricky Show* (1956-1958), in which he played a busboy; and *Action Theater* (1962-1965), in which he worked with Johnny Ginger.

On some levels, Romig's *Ricky the Clown* television persona wasn't much of a stretch. A native Detroiter, both parents worked in the circus—dad with Ringling Bros., mom with the The Riding Rooneys. Romig followed his parents into the family profession at age 5, when he linked with the Frank McIntyre Circus. The Romig family later fused into the Romig and Rooney Circus. According to the www.detroitkidshow.com Web site, the circus claimed "Trained Horses, Educated Mules, Trick Dogs, Clever Ponies, Acrobats, Bareback Riders, Jugglers, Wire Walkers, Aerialists, Trick Roping and Clowns, Clowns, Clowns!"

Romig described his motivation for pursuing a show business career in "The Show Goes On," his autobiography: "If I could do something that was a little outstanding, that nobody else could do, I took pride in that. I think that got into my head through the circus. Anytime I found something that I could do that others couldn't, that made me real happy … inside and all over."

Channel 7's Ricky the Clown.

## Sacto, Sgt. (a.k.a. Tom Ryan)

He amused Channel 50 viewers in the late 1960s and 1970 with his "double pumper" salute and *Little Rascals* reruns. Tom Ryan's show-biz resume before Sgt. Sacto's debut in the summer of 1967 was slim. He had worked in the mailroom at WKNR-AM and wrote one-liners in Channel 50's promotion department—lines like "Watch Lucy and Ethel as they go to the chocolate factory." Prior to unveiling his first "double pumper" salute, Ryan

Sgt. Sacto demonstrates the "double pumper" salute.

spent a summer playing basketball in Europe (where he played against former Democratic presidential candidate Bill Bradley in a game at the Royal Albert Hall). While in Copenhagen on his basketball excursion, Ryan picked up an odd, spacey-looking running suit that was to come in handy later.

Two things happened upon Ryan's return from Europe: Johnny Ginger lost interest in doing his afternoon kiddie show on Channel 50 and Ryan was tapped to take over in 1967. (Only weeks before, during the 1967 riots, as part of his duties with the Air National Guard, he protected Hot Sam's on Gratiot Avenue with an unloaded rifle.) Ryan dug out his running suit from Copenhagen, painted his eyebrows up like the Mr. Spock character from *Star Trek* and kicked off "*The Captain Detroit Show*, starring Sgt. Sacto." The show consisted of Ryan hosting *Little Rascals* and *Three Stooges* reruns, plus Hanna-Barbera cartoons. Sacto became a cult hit among college students. However, the show began imploding year by year. What started out as a 90-minute program in 1967 had shrunk to 30 minutes by the time Ryan was laid off during a companywide budget-cutting move in 1970. The double-pumper salute was to be seen no more. And Ryan went on to a successful radio career—first with Dick Purtan on WXYZ-AM, and eventually at WOMC-FM.

## Sales, Soupy

In 50 years of Detroit television, he is Detroit's most recognizable and original star. Baby Boomers remember having lunch with Soupy, along with sidekicks White Fang and Black Tooth. Boomer parents remember Sales' late night program. Sales' guest list for the late night show included jazz greats Charlie Parker, Miles Davis and Duke Ellington. No discussion about Channel 7 would be complete without him.

Before he became Soupy, Milton Supman (also known as Milton Hines) worked in Cleveland and Cincinnati. In Cleveland,

"Hey kids, last night was New Year's Eve, and your mother and dad were out having a great time. They are probably still sleeping and what I want you to do is tip-toe in their bedroom and go in your mom's pocketbook and your dad's pants, which are probably on the floor. You'll see lots of green pieces of paper with pictures of guys in beards. Put them in an envelope and send them to me at Soupy Sales, Channel 5, New York, New York. And you know what I'm going to send you? A post card from Puerto Rico!"

Soupy Sales, as a young man.

he was a contemporary of Alan Freed—generally considered the most important rock deejay of his era. Sales also hosted *Soupy's Soda Shop*, one of the first TV teen dance shows. Sales came north looking for work, going for auditions at WJR-AM, CKLW-AM, and WJBK-AM. "None of 'em wanted me," he recalled later.

But in 1953, Channel 7 general manager John Pival took one look at the young comic and decided the station *did* want Soupy. Pival renamed him Soupy Sales (because, Pival thought, the name "Hines" would scare off potential food sponsors) and gave him an afternoon slot in 1953. The result was some of the most memorable television in Detroit history. *Lunch With Soupy* started out with manic piano music, followed by Sales' joshing with White Fang (an unruly dog with a deep voice) and Black Tooth ("the sweetest dog in all of Deetroit"). Both were played by Clyde Adler.

Soupy Sales gets help "killing" a hot dog from White Fang.

Channel 9's Larry Sands.

Herkimer the Dragon and Cecil B. Rabbit.

Soupy became so big that the ABC-TV network used the show as a five-night-a-week summer replacement show in 1955—perhaps the only network television show to originate live from this city. Sales also did a late night show that ran at 11 p.m. in lieu of news. He never got credit for it, but Sales had much to do with keeping jazz on the radar in Detroit. He featured alto saxophonist Charlie Parker on the program twice. Miles Davis made an appearance. So did Duke Ellington. It was a breakneck pace—two shows a day, five days a week. Recalls Sales: "I was meeting myself coming and going." He kept up the pace for seven years, until 1960.

Sales' career after that was checkered. He hosted kid shows in Los Angeles and New York, appeared with the rock group Sha Na Na in their syndicated comic TV program and hosted a radio show on New York's WNBC-AM. Most of the tapes of his old shows are gone, but a few survive. There's a booming business for them via the Internet. Sales has the rights to those recordings, and tours with his old work products. Detroit is still his hottest market.

### Sands, Larry (d: 1974)

He was the multi-talented comedic cyclone behind Channel 9's *Jingles In Boofland*. Sands produced the show, composed the *Jingles In Boofland* theme music, wrote the jokes, voiced the puppets Herkimer the Dragon and Cecil B. Rabbit W.G.A. (World's Great Authority) and appeared occasionally on air. Sands would have gone on to become a player in Detroit TV, had he not been fired during one of CKLW-TV's pointless personnel purges in the mid-1960s. Had he not died in a helicopter crash in southern California in 1974, Sands might have become a force in Hollywood.

Born January 22, 1932, Sands (real name: Lester Solomon) grew up in Chicago and attended the University of Illinois where he majored in music. Like many who worked in early Detroit television, the road to Detroit ran through various smaller radio and television stations. Sands hosted *Larry Sands' Big League News and Chatter* in Erie, Pennsylvania. He met Jerry Booth (who went on to play Jingles) at a Fort Wayne, Indiana, television station. Booth had worked at the station as a clown. Booth and Sands created a jester character who lived in a castle. *Jingles* debuted in the 5-6 p.m. slot on Channel 9 in 1959 as *Looney Tunes and Jingles In Boofland*. Channel 9 dropped the "Looney Tunes" part the following year. It lasted until 1963. *The Larry and Jerry Show* ran for approximately one year afterward.

There is little that Sands couldn't do, either on the air or off. Perhaps his most famous character was a supercilious ornithologist whose bird calls—no matter what the bird—always sounded the same: "Twaaa. ...Twaaa." His Boofland characters included Mr. Binki, the postman. On *Larry and Jerry*, the post-Boofland show that aired in the 5 p.m. weekday time slot on Channel 9, he played Emma Frettersby and the artist Grbtz, who always painted the same picture. He occasionally filled in for Bill Kennedy at the movie desk and did weather at night. Off air, he and pizza mogul Mike Ilitch were friends. In fact, Sands owned a half-dozen Little Caesars franchises when he lived here in Detroit, and liked to hang out at downtown Detroit's Lindell AC.

The story of Sands' Channel 9 firing, as told by his widow, Marian, of Beverly Hills, California, is an old one: A new program director decided Sands' $25,000-a-year salary was too much. Sands left Detroit for Chicago, where he worked at the Leo Burnett ad agency. Four years later, he moved to Hollywood, where his talents had room to grow. He wrote for Tim Conway, Sonny and Cher, Phyllis Diller, Larry Storch and Jimmy Durante, and also composed music for Sea World, Marineland and Magic Mountain. At the time of his death, he was writing a film for his buddy, Tony Curtis.

### The Jingles in Boofland theme:

Away across the Ishkabow,
And across the Foofram Sea,
There is a place called Boofland,
Where very soon you'll be.
Boofland is full of surprises,
Like birds and dragons and things,
And inside the magic castle,
Jingles laughs, dances and sings.

### The Boofland anthem:

Oh Boofland, my Boofland
Let us always sing.
And have some fun with Cecil B.
Herkimer and Jing.
No matter how big I get.
No matter where I go.
I'll always watch my TV set
For the Jingles Show.
The Jingles Show.

Channel 2's Sagebrush Shorty.

## Shorty, Sagebrush (d: 1999)

Ventriloquist Sagebrush Shorty (real name: Ted Lloyd) hosted cartoons, performed magic tricks and jested with his two dummies, Bronco Billy Buttons and Skinny Duggan.

Each show began and ended with a tape of Sagebrush riding a horse amid wide-open western sagebrush. He appeared in western garb that included a cowboy hat and a glittery tie. It gave him the look of a boisterous broncobuster—a character he created somewhere between 1947 and 1949 when he worked in Los Angeles. Magic ran in the family: His father, Byron Lloyd (known as Elmore the Great), was a fabled Texas show-biz figure. His lore includes the story of how Elmore kept his act going one night despite suffering an attack of appendicitis. (The malady got the better of him at the end of the act when Elmore couldn't straighten up while taking a bow. He was rushed to the hospital, where he recovered.) Before the younger Lloyd was even 20, he was writing a show, *Famous Trials of History*, at an L.A. radio station.

Sagebrush Shorty had been a children's television star (also doing news) in San Antonio, Texas, during the early and mid 1950s before moving to Detroit in 1955. (George B. Storer had owned the station in San Antonio, but sold it and moved Sagebrush to Detroit, where he debuted *Sagebrush Shorty and His Circle 2 Theater* in the 5-6 p.m. weekday slot. He also ran *Cartoon Classroom*, which featured visits each Tuesday and Friday from Sgt. Dusty Rhodes, who lectured on safety.)

What strikes a viewer of Sagebrush Shorty's show is the gentle, guileless nature of Shorty's act. One of the few remaining tapes of the show has Shorty performing the day before Easter Sunday, 1959. He introduced members of a Cub Scout and Girl Scout troop, accepted a cake from one of his fans, brought on a rabbit and the owner of a pet store who explained the ins and outs of keeping rabbits as pets, and refereed an egg-rolling contest.

There were eight characters on the show, in addition to the

famed Skinny Dugan: Sir Reginald, Ringo, Little Theethill (that's Cecil with a lisp), Dee Dee the Deer, Billy Buffalo, Count R. Clockwise, and the Professor. Sagebrush moonlighted, too: He owned the Sagebrush Shorty School of Dance, Music and Affiliated Arts, in Center Line. Sagebrush worked at Channel 2 between 1955 and 1960 and then at Channel 7 in the 11 a.m. Saturday slot in 1962. He returned to Los Angeles sometime in the late 1960s. He was a bartender in his later years, and died in 1999.

What really thrilled the children was Shorty's "pyramid of prizes," a pile of toys he'd hand out to lucky attendees of the show. And he would sign off with the words: "Y'all be kind to each other."

## Welch, Marv

Welch was testimony to the fact that a good performer can play any part. During the 1950s and 1960s, Welch was one of the area's busiest nightclub comics. He worked with everybody from Frank Sinatra to Jerry Vale. Blue jokes were his specialty. That was at night. During the day, 7-8 a.m., he was Wixie on Channel 7's *Wixie's Wonderland*. He'd appear in a toga with a large "7" on the front, a large gold belt and a beanie with a television antenna on top.

The show had it all: Diane Dale, an accomplished pianist and organist, played and sang kiddie songs. Frank Nastasi, appearing as "Gramps," would bring various animals on the show. Rounding out the cast was Ken Muse, who played "Gee Whiz, the Fastest Artist There Is."

The fit between Welch's evening existence as an adult comic and daytime work as a kiddie show host was not as strange as it seemed. Welch taught music to grade schoolers earlier in his career. And then, there was the concept of professionalism. "When you're in a show, you play the part," he said in an interview. "If you're a comic telling dirty jokes, that's what you do. If you're entertaining children, that's what you do. You simply control yourself."

*What follows is from a 1959 Hires Root Beer promotional decal designed to be affixed to the back window of the family station wagon:*

SAGEBRUSH SHORTY'S
BACKSEAT RIDER'S
CLUB RULES

I WILL

Ride only in back seat.
Not play in car.
Not raise my voice in car.
Obey the driver of car.
Always practice safety rules.

HIRES TO YOU!

# Hosts
## and Programs

*One showed us home movies of the world. Another spent a few years in Hollywood and then talked about it for decades. What would Detroit have been without George Pierrot and Bill Kennedy? These are the people who gave Detroit television its personality.*

## Allen, Ed

Allen put television viewers through their paces on Channel 4 between the late 1950s and early 1970s, and was considered one of the country's first TV exercisemeisters. And he pumped up ratings. During some periods in the early 1960s, three out of every four television sets switched on during the 9:30 a.m. time period were switched to *Ed Allen Time*. He appeared with Lorene Babcock and Carol Duvall later in the decade.

There was a lot more to Ed Allen than muscle. At one time, he sang opera with the Chicago Civic Opera Company, worked as a comedian in Detroit-area supper clubs just after World War II and even auditioned for the part of "Tarzan."

After leaving Channel 4, Allen's early entrepreneurial adventures developed. He wrote a comic strip entitled *The Adventures of Ed Allen*, opened a chain of health clubs in Canada, and generally turned his own sweat into wealth.

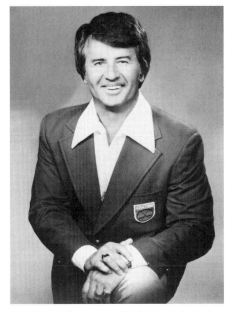

Ed Allen: The man with the muscles.

*Bowling for Dollars* host Bob Allison.

Sonny Eliot was host, but *At the Zoo's* real stars were from the animal kingdom.

## Allison, Bob

He is mostly known as the host of radio's *Ask Your Neighbor,* which has been on Detroit's airwaves since 1962. But Allison (real name, Bob Allesee) also helmed Channel 4's *Bowling For Dollars,* which he hosted with Regis Philbin-like insouciance.

A native of Indiana, Allison's career took several twists. He played jazz piano in Los Angeles; worked at WWJ-AM radio, where *Ask Your Neighbor* aired between 1962 and 1978, as a host; and then took *Neighbor* to various other Detroit radio stations. As of this writing, the show could be heard at WNZK-AM.

Allison's ratings as host of *Bowling For Dollars* between 1973 and 1979 were amazing. In fact, Allison liked bowling. He bowled with three teams—the Detroit Athletic Club, Detroit Rotary Club and Oakland Hills Country Club. But he hated doing the show for two reasons: A week's episodes of *Bowling For Dollars* were shot on Friday, meaning he'd have to haul five changes of clothing to an Allen Park bowling alley each Friday night. "I'm the kind of guy who likes getting up for work," he said in an interview. "But on Fridays, I'd get up and realize I had to do three hours of *Ask Your Neighbor* and then five *Bowling For Dollars.* I would become nauseous." In addition, the show had little in the way of backstage production help. "I like to think I made it look easy," he said later, "but it wasn't."

Years later, he still becomes irritated when people describe bowling as an exclusively blue-collar sport. "I bowled for years with the guys from the DAC (one of Detroit's best clubs) and I never saw any of them with a lunch bucket or a blue collar. Most of them could've bought and sold Channel 4 (the station that cancelled *Bowling For Dollars*) if they felt like it."

## At the Zoo

Sonny Eliot (also see "Weather" chapter) hosted this charming weekly exploration of the Detroit Zoo. It aired between 1962 and 1979, and starred various creatures at Detroit's zoo—even airing during the winter, when, at that time, the zoo wasn't open to the public. Eliot would explain what the animals ate and how fast they ran. Guests would sometimes drop by. One night, Colonel Sanders made an appearance.

Shooting this show was not without its dangers. During the show's 17-year history, Eliot was urinated on by a rhinoceros, spat on by a llama and bitten by a goose. And this doesn't include jokes the technical crew would play on him. Often, they would slip garter snakes into Eliot's suit pockets.

## Bahr, Betty

She was omnipresent during local TV's early days, especially when all of the commercials and programming were live. Bahr appeared on some 17 shows during her career, which stretched from the 1950s into the early 1970s. Her credits included five shows each on Channels 2, 4 and 7, plus two on Channel 9.

Consider her schedule for a time: She would wrap up her work doing commercials on Channels 4's *Time For Music with Sammy Diebert* at 6:15 p.m. A waiting car took her immediately to Channel 2's New Center-area studios, where she would do commercials for Jac Le Goff's 6:25 p.m. newscast. "Every now and then, somebody would ask me: 'Do you know somebody is imitating you? She even wears the same clothes.'"

Bahr grew up in Detroit, getting her early performing experience at Detroit's Civic Light Opera. Her early television credits included *Shadow Stumpers*, a Channel 4 game show that Bahr hosted with Sonny Eliot, and *Conversations with Todd Purse and Friends.* The show featured conversation between host Purse and—surprise!—various friends. Bahr was among the friends.

J.D. Beemer: Justice Colt.

After leaving show business, she raised seven children in her Harper Woods home. Decades after leaving the medium, people still recognize her.

## Beemer, J.D.

He introduced western movies on Channel 7 as "Justice Colt" during the early 1950s. Beemer was the son of Brace Beemer (d: 1965), who played both Sergeant Preston of the Yukon and The Lone Ranger on WXYZ radio. Although the younger Beemer's family connections undoubtedly got him the job as Justice Colt, that wasn't the only consideration. Channel 7 chieftain John Pival originally planned to hire Beemer's older brother, but settled on the younger Beemer when J.D. exhibited skill in handling a horse on the Beemer family farm in Oakland County.

## Bell, Rita (d. 2003)

During the 1960s, her daily *Prize Movie* placed Rita Bell among the first rank of Detroit TV personalities. Each weekday at 8:30 a.m., she'd introduce a movie (which she would show in its entirety), play a tune for her audience and ask viewers to call in with the song title. The viewer who answered correctly would get Bell's prize—$7, although the pot sometimes rolled over to more serious proportions.

A graduate of Marygrove College, where she studied drama, Bell began her career as a public relations representative at the United Foundation. On occasion, she sang with big bands in Detroit. One evening, while attending a function for the now-defunct Wrigley's supermarket chain, Channel 7 general manager John Pival heard her sing with a group of strolling musicians and invited her to stop by for an interview. Bell was reluctant at first, but was told that the UF did a lot of business with Channel 7 and that she ought to take up Pival's invitation. She did. He hired her as a "weather girl," but for a difficult shift—12:25 a.m., fol-

Rita Bell with her omnipresent telephone.

lowing *Lou Gordon's Hotseat*. For a while, her schedule consisted of working an eight-hour day, going home for a nap, and reporting to Channel 7 for her post-midnight weather gig. It wasn't easy.

Within three years, Channel 7 put her behind the desk—where she stayed until well into the 1970s. Bell was magnificently chipper—so chipper and wholesome, in fact, she made June Cleaver seem like Joan Crawford.

Television changed during the 1970s. Nothing exemplifies the way TV became homogenized from coast-to-coast than the way *Prize Movie* was whittled away to nothing and eventually taken off the air. ABC Inc., which owned Channel 7 and four other stations, wanted standard programming in each of its five owned-and-operated stations. It was pretty much the same show with a different name, depending on the city—*AM New York, AM Los Angeles, AM Chicago*, etc. Detroit, of course, had to have *AM Detroit*. The idea of a movie in the morning became an outdated concept, and was replaced by talk shows like Phil Donahue. Bell continued until 1978, when she was given the ziggy after 21 years. She now lives in San Diego.

## Bergeson, Chuck

Bergeson hosted *Ladies' Day*, Channel 2's morning show, throughout the 1950s. The biggest stars of the era, including Lucille Ball, Jerry Lewis and Red Buttons, were interviewed on this one-hour program. *Ladies' Day* also featured games, stunts and prizes, all performed before a live audience. And there was a marriage, too. Bergeson and Margaret Tomaney, who sang on the program, were hitched in June 1954.

He started out in radio in Sault Ste. Marie and Flint before hiring on at Channel 2 in 1952. The regular *Ladies' Day* host went on vacation during the summer of 1952. Bergeson filled in—until 1959. In addition, Bergeson worked as the station's news direc-

No, that's not Drew Carey. It's *Ladies' Day* host Chuck Bergeson.

tor, host of *Your TV Golf Pro*, and *The Name Game*, Channel 2's game show.

Bergeson left the air in 1959 for an off-air job in station management. He later managed the Storer Broadcasting station in Cleveland, and stations in Norfolk, Virginia., and San Jose, California. Retired, he now lives in California.

## Chiappetta, Jerry

While Mort Neff was the television medium's pioneer outdoorsman, Chiappetta represents the second generation. Chiappetta was on the air from 1968 to 1977 with some 800 shows, and hosted *Michigan Outdoors* after Neff's retirement.

Chiappetta's roots ran in print journalism. He was the United Press International night editor before joining the *Detroit Free Press* during the late 1960s as an outdoor writer. It was a dream job, but Channel 7 officials came calling with their checkbook. Channel 7 general manager John Campbell, noting that Channel 4 had Mort Neff in its stable, wanted an outdoors show. The offer: Campbell would double Chiappetta's *Free Press* pay from $12,500 to $25,000 if he would join the station. Chiappetta gave the *Free Press* three weeks' notice, but was asked to leave immediately.

Chiappetta was quite high profile for the next four years. He appeared on Channel 7's morning variety show on Thursdays discussing outdoor-related topics; would appear later during the day with Bill Bonds on the station's afternoon newscast; and hosted *Michigan Sportsman* at 6:30 p.m. Saturdays. Five other television stations eventually picked up the show statewide.

However, Channel 7 hired Neff back a few years later, and Chiappetta shuffled off briefly to Channel 9. Neff later came calling with a deal in 1972. Over lunch in Southfield, Neff told Chiappetta that he (Neff) would retire in a year. Chiappetta could buy out Neff, and become the Mort Neff of the new generation. Chiappetta agreed, producing new *Michigan Outdoors* programs

*Michigan Outdoors* host Jerry Chiappetta hunted wildlife with his camera.

until 1976. With the exception of *Michigan Family Outdoors*, which ran for 18 episodes in 1980, Chiappetta was more or less through with local broadcasting.

Since leaving Detroit, Chiappetta has had a successful run doing what he did here in the Motor City. He hosted *Hunting Strategies* on ESPN; *Sports Afield* for cable television; and *Jeep Outdoors* for Michigan's Jeep dealers. He now lives in Maryland, where he owns wildharvestvideos.com.

## Curtis, Minnie Jo

Long before Jack Paar, Johnny Carson and Jay Leno, Channel 4 aired its own late night talk show. Alternately entitled *The Minnie Jo Show* and *Late Date*, hostess Minnie Jo Curtis served up pleasant chat and celebrity interviews in the early 1950s, weeknights at 11:30 p.m. "You'd have celebrities visiting Detroit for any number of reasons. Most of the time, I think, they were visiting to pick up cars," she recalled. As far as can be determined, she was the first Detroit television personality to "go network."

Producer Walt Koste originally hired Curtis in 1944 as a writer for WWJ-AM's *The Coffee Club*, a morning radio gabfest. During the 1940s and 1950s, actors and actresses could find plentiful work in local radio, local television, and summer theatre. Curtis could be heard on *The Green Hornet* and *The Lone Ranger*, or seen at Channel 4. (She also worked in Chicago and New York, grabbing whatever acting work she could find.) She starred in the DuMont Network's *Shopper's Matinee*, a daily variety show that aired midafternoon. She is retired and lives with her husband, Carl, in New Mexico.

## Davis, Johnny "Scat" (d: 1983)

Davis sang, played trumpet and led a band at Channel 7 during the early 1950s. *Jazz Nocturne* (1951), *Coffee and Cakes* (1951-52) and *Starlit Stairway* all featured Davis—who was already famous by the time he joined Channel 7. It was Davis who sang "Hooray For Hollywood," Tinseltown's anthem, in the 1930s-era film, *Hollywood Hotel*.

An Indiana native and third-generation musician, Davis' grandfather ran the Royal British Navy Band. Getting his first professional job at age 13, Davis found work with Fred Waring, Red Nichols and others before embarking on a successful Hollywood career. He had 15 films to his credit. He retired to Texas, where he died of a heart attack on a hunting trip. His papers can be found at Texas Tech University.

## Detroit Tubeworks

Local television's first nod to the counterculture of the late 1960s, *Detroit Tubeworks* was to the young audiences of the day what *Backstage Pass* was to audiences of the 1990s: a place for progressive music artists to be heard. Viewers might see WABX air ace Dave Dixon (d: 1999) interviewing poet Allen Ginsberg (d: 1997); catch performances by groups as varied as Captain Beefheart, Fleetwood Mac (before they became pop music idols), or Earth, Wind & Fire; or see random industrial film footage employed as a visual backdrop to a song by the Eric Clapton-fronted rock group, Cream. Once, the producers showed *Paths of Glory*, the classic Stanley Kubrick antiwar film. This was television at its hippest, circa the late 1960s.

*Tubeworks* was an outgrowth of *Live From Planet Earth* on Channel 56. A few video freaks at Wayne State University persuaded the station to keep the program on in another form. The show was later moved to WXON-TV after sponsors—usually local head shops and boutiques—agreed to advertise.

The production of the show bears mentioning: The show's hosts and production team would trundle over to WXON-TV's Walled Lake studios, usually after midnight, and shoot while everybody else was away. "They told us, 'Well, nobody else is using the studio, so go on make a television show,'" recalls Chuck Riti, who worked as an editor on the show.

The producers were allowed total creative freedom. Hosting this show were the WABX-FM "air aces"—a crowd of hip, young men (they were all men) who were in the vanguard of changing musical tastes of the time. Dixon, Dan Carlisle, Jerry Lubin and Mark Parenteau could be seen. Local rock groups such as the MC5 could be both seen and heard. The show also propelled WABX newsman Harvey Ovshinsky into a television career.

## Dixon, Dave (d: 1999)

Although known mostly as a radio host, Dixon did some television work in his native Detroit: He hosted an interview show briefly on Channel 38 during the late 1980s. He would have done more, except there seemed to no longer be room for an eccentric but talented character like Dixon on the local tube.

Dixon became locally famous as a WABX "air ace" during the late 1960s and early 1970s, and worked on *Detroit Tubeworks*, a Channel 56 program that explored hip underground cultural and news topics. He quit WABX to become an overnight movie host at a Ft. Lauderdale television station during the 1970s, and became a southern Florida cult figure. In a pattern that repeated itself throughout his life, Dixon had trouble with his bosses in Florida—although, the trouble wasn't always his fault. Once, one of his employers stumbled in during Dixon's TV show and offered to play a "game" with Dixon during a commercial break. "You hit me as hard as you can. But then, if I get up, I hit you." Dixon declined, and quit within a few weeks. He was rehired at the same station when commercial revenue evaporated.

A case of Bell's Palsy ended Dixon's Florida TV career, and sent him to his hometown in the north. He worked at WDET-FM, at Channel 38, and finally at WXYT-AM, where he was employed when he died in 1999.

## Duvall, Carol

Duvall conducted celebrity interviews and meted out fashion tips on Channel 4's *Living* program during the 1960s. The show also featured muscleman Ed Allen and Lorene Babcock. It was a blend of Martha Stewart, Richard Simmons and Rosie O'Donnell—crafts, exercise and celebrity interviews. At varying times during her 14-year career at Channel 4 (1962-1976), Duvall did just about everything. She anchored the noon news with Ted Russell, hosted a five-minute program that aired between George Pierrot's *World Adventure Series* and Channel 4's early newscast, and helmed a five-minute crafts program during early afternoons.

Although she perpetually looked about age 40, Duvall was a pioneering figure in Michigan TV. Educated at Michigan State University and New York University, she began work at Grand Rapids' WOOD-TV (which also gave us Al Ackerman) in 1951, not long after the station went on the air. Her resume also included programs such as *Chit Chat*, *Carol and Alex* and *The Miss Michigan Pageant*. By the time she arrived at Channel 4 in 1962, she was probably the most seasoned female broadcaster in the state.

*Living* went off the air and Duvall left town during the mid-1970s. She recovered remarkably well, and now can be seen nationally on cable's HGTV network, where she anchors a crafts show. She is known nationally as "The Queen of Crafts." And she still maintains a home in Bear Lake, Michigan, not far from Traverse City.

## Farr, Mel

The jingle "Mel Farr superstar…for a far-r-r-r better deal" ran on Detroit television for more than 20 years, from the late 1970s until the early 2000s. The ad campaign featured the cape-clad. ex-

NFL star Farr, flying Superman-like through the air. Farr and television newsman Jerry Blocker came up with the idea, according to former Detroit newswoman Charlene Mitchell. "They were calling him superstar on the field—that was his nickname—so Mel and Jerry decided to play off of it," recalled Mitchell, who worked for Farr and helped produce the spots.

Farr grew up in Texas and played college football at UCLA before joining the Detroit Lions as a number one draft pick in 1967. He remained with the team through 1973. Three decades after his last game, Farr's stats still place him among the Top 10 Lions running backs of all time: 3,072 yards gained in 739 carries, 26 touchdowns (including nine touchdowns during the 1970 season); and a 197-yard game against the Minnesota Vikings on November 12, 1967.

He was a great success after football—for a time. Farr trained with the Ford Motor Co. during the off season, opening his own dealerships after his retirement from football. The local ad campaign made him famous. *Black Enterprise* magazine identified Farr's company as the biggest African-American-owned business in the country in 1986. The company that year reported sales of $596.6 million. His dealership empire later went into an eclipse and folded in 2002.

People may or may not remember Farr's success or his failure. But they remember the outfit. "He was a prisoner of that cape," says Mitchell.

## Friedman, Sonya

This psychologist hosted a talk show on WDIV-TV during the 1980s before joining CNN as the host of *Sonya Live*.

Friedman earned a doctorate in psychology from Wayne State University before turning into a one-woman, multimedia conglomerate. Her credits include a decade on radio, magazine articles and five books, including *Men Are Just Desserts* and *Smart*

**Another Detroit classic: The lyrics to the Roy O'Brien ad jingle, said to be the longest-running ad jingle.**

Stay on the right track
To Nine Mile and Mack
Roy O'Brien trucks and cars
Make your money back.

Roy O'Brien's got them buyin'
And buyin'
They come
From many miles away.
You'll save yourself
A lot of dollars, and dollars
By driving out his way today.

So stay on the right track
To Nine Mile and Mack
To get the best deal in town.
'Cause Roy O'Brien's
Got the best deal around.

*Cookies Don't Crumble.*

Her Channel 4 program, which ran during the early 1980s, featured a combination of newsmaker interviews and self-help talk. In some ways its content resembled Oprah Winfrey's show—uplifting and intelligent, with an occasional freak thrown in to make things interesting. Oprah hit the air after Friedman left Channel 4 and took the formula to the stratosphere. (Indeed, Diane Hudson—one of Friedman's producers—later went to work for Winfrey.)

Friedman's work was good enough to land her at the Cable News Network, where she hosted *Sonya Live*. The CNN show went off the air in 1994 after seven years.

## Hamtramck

*Hamtramck* was created as a half-hour spoof of Detroit's east side, but ended up signaling the end of local entertainment programming in Detroit. Written in 1987 by Channel 4's Tom De Lisle, a Detroit native, the program was to have been a send-up of all of the goofy weddings De Lisle had attended as a youngster growing up near Detroit's Gratiot/McNichols neighborhood. De Lisle's original script told the story of a young woman from a fancy Bloomfield Hills address marrying a young man from the working class east side.

De Lisle had the idea of humorously exploring the immutable division between east siders and west siders—an open joke among Detroit residents. WOMC-FM's Tom Ryan, who had worked with De Lisle on nine Count Scary projects, was cast as the father of the bride. Socialite Tom Schoenith and Detroit Tiger manager Sparky Anderson made cameo appearances. Annette Sinclair, who was married to rock star Bob Seger at the time, played the bride. Not long before filming, Channel 4 officials changed the name of the program from *East Side/West Side* to *Hamtramck*. De Lisle later recalled that "red flags were going up all over the place. But nobody wanted to listen."

*Hamtramck* included a polka band playing "Proud Mary" and a 15-year-old throwing up in the parking lot—hardly unusual sights at weddings anywhere. It also showed a woman filching a centerpiece from one of the tables. De Lisle's own mother, Virginia, played the woman.

The problem was that some took the program as an attack on Polish-Americans. Egged on by the title, the mayors of Hamtramck and Warren demanded an apology from the station—and got one from Channel 4 General Manager Amy McCombs. Hamtramck Mayor Robert Kozaren said, "it was an insult to Polish-American womanhood." McCombs appeared with Kozaren at a press conference and issued a public *mea culpa*—even though plenty of Polish-Americans thought the show was dead-bang accurate and not at all insulting. Absent the controversy, the show conceivably could have developed into a weekly, locally produced sitcom. However, the bleating from the politicians killed the idea. "The entire thing was surreal," De Lisle later recalled. And although the ratings were huge, Channel 4 virtually removed itself from the business of doing local entertainment programming after *Hamtramck*.

## Harris, Fran (d: 1998)

She was a pioneer in both Detroit radio and television. Harris, who joined WWJ-AM in 1930, was said to be the first woman radio newscaster in Michigan. After establishing herself on the radio, particularly with her wartime newscasts, she later became the first woman ever to appear on Detroit TV when she appeared on Channel 4 during its debut broadcast of October 23, 1946. After that, her reputation only grew. As evidence of her esteem in 1960, some 200 women showed up at a surprise party in downtown Detroit's Veterans Memorial Building to celebrate her 30 years on the air.

There was little Harris couldn't do. She could read the news. She could host virtually anything on television *or* radio—soft or serious. When radio was a baby medium not taken seriously by anybody, she was a local star with programs such as *Julia Hayes' Household Hints* (1931-1935) and *Nancy Dixon Store News* (1939-1942). But she could do a lot more than fluff. While many of the male newscasters were off fighting during World War II, she became WWJ-AM's first female newscaster. She won a Peabody Award—the broadcasting equivalent of a Pulitzer Prize—for a series she did on sex criminals during the late 1940s.

Later, after television became a serious medium, she developed *Junior Jamboree* (a children's program) and was a star of TV's *Traffic Court*, for which she wore blue makeup because cameras didn't pick up red very well in those days. Her career lasted until the mid-1970s. Harris died in a Livonia nursing home in 1998.

## Hit A Homer

An early 1950s game show hosted by Channel 4's Sonny Eliot, contestants would move up a "base" if they answered a question correctly. Especially difficult questions earned players more than one base. Sometimes, when producers couldn't find enough contestants, they went to the nearby Adams Bar to round up participants. Often that included drunken *Detroit News* employees.

The game show went off the air after a single season, probably because the baseball strategy was a bit too involved.

## Hynes, Bob

He hosted *The Morning Show* on Channel 7 between 1966 and 1977—a 90-minute daily variety show that featured everything from cooking segments to child-rearing advice to music. Pianist Matt Michaels fronted a trio. Psychologist Sonya Friedman made her first television appearance here, as did Jerry Baker. Both went on to successful television careers.

*The Morning Show's* Bob Hynes.

Hynes' genial style played well, and took him on to other TV and radio engagements after leaving Channel 7. He hosted movies on Channel 9 after Bill Kennedy left for Channel 50; hosted the statewide lottery show; and then worked at WJR-AM for 15 years, between 1975 and 1990. He still does occasional on-air work in town.

## Jarkey, Harry

Jarkey hosted one of Detroit's early talk shows, *Our Friend Harry*, which aired during the 9:30 to 11:30 a.m. slot on Channel 7 between 1959 and 1961. The show featured interviews with various guests as they'd come through town. Those included everybody from Chuck Connors of *The Rifleman* fame to the King of Sweden. Local regulars included Marv Welch, Jean Loach and newsman Dick Femmel.

Although Jarkey did little comedy on the show, he was a stand-up comic by training. A sample joke: "They say a single man dies before a married man … so get married and have a slow death." A native of Nashville, he arrived in Depression-era Detroit and started a career in the town's nightclubs. Jarkey was a regular at Windsor's Elmwood Casino and long-forgotten clubs such as the Club 509. He later worked the casino at Wenona Beach, near Bay City, between Memorial Day and Labor Day for some 25 years. He kept the Bay City engagement, commuting daily between Bay City and Broadcast House in Southfield during the summer.

Now in his 90s, he lives in southern California.

## Lezell, Maurice (a.k.a. Mr. Belvedere)

Long before Lee Iacocca took to the air to pitch Chryslers, there was Mr. Belvedere (real name: Maurice Lezell). His advertising spots were among the most famous on 1960s-era television. The phrase "We do good work" became part of

Detroit's cultural fabric. So did "Have no fear with Belvedere," and "You'll look at it, you'll love it, you'll take your time paying for it."

Mr. Belvedere entered the home improvement business in the early 1950s. He made his first advertising foray on radio. "It was Mother's Day," he recalled. "The host at WJLB invited me down to the station to wish everybody happy Mother's Day. I was kidding around. I said, 'A beautiful mother's day gift would be a new kitchen. Here's the number. Tyler 87100.' I came in the next morning and my phone was ringing like crazy." He later moved his homespun campaigns to television, making his pitches on late night television immediately after the new medium was born. "We blew every remodeling company off the air," he remembered.

He later became a regular with Bill Kennedy and Conrad Patrick, and sponsored late night movies on Channel 2. "I was the first one to realize the impact, the power of someone representing their own company on TV. Where I made out is that I put all the money back into TV."

Lezell broke the ice for people like Mel Farr and Ollie Fretter. Says Lezell: "I was the first one to throw the stone."

Maurice Lezell: He does good work.

**These are the lyrics to the Mr. Belvedere home improvement commercials:**

Here's the magic number
Keep it by your side.
Belvedere Construction.
They are known both far and wide.
For the best in home improvement
They're known throughout the state.
Call Tyler 8-7100 for a home improvement date.

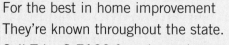

## Kennedy, Bill (d: 1997)

He was easily Detroit's most distinctive movie host. From 1956 until 1983, Kennedy brought a head full of Hollywood trivia—gained from working for 15 years in the movie business in California—to viewers who sat through classic and sometimes not-so-classic movies. He was amusing, sometimes arrogant, but always fascinating to watch. He'd signal for the director to return to the movie with a wave of the hand, fiddle with his glasses, take viewer questions, talk about the old days and the stars he knew—which seemed to be everyone from Humphrey Bogart to John Barrymore. Sometimes he seemed like a berserk old duke, sometimes the bard of the silver screen. Wrote Mike Mosher in *Cinegram* magazine: "Kennedy's gestures are those of a sage at a cocktail party, answering queries as much for the fun of it as for information." He was also a prankster, once calling Hudson's lingerie department to see if they carried any "Freudian slips." Channel 9 viewers saw him from 1956 until 1969, when he moved to Channel 50 until 1983.

A native of Cleveland, Kennedy first arrived in Detroit during the 1930s as an announcer and newsman on WWJ-AM. Tall and impressive looking, he thought he'd give Hollywood a try. Thousands of young men would come to Hollywood hoping to become the next Bogart or Barrymore. Most would fail miserably. Kennedy didn't fail. But he didn't succeed wildly, either. He appeared in 60 movies—most of them "B" films that showed up after midnight on television when TV still programmed old movies.

During his time in Hollywood, Kennedy got to work with some of the greats, including Bette Davis (in *Now Voyager*) and Cary Grant (in *Destination Tokyo*). He even appeared in *Joan of Arc*, saying, "Throw another faggot on the fire." It's Kennedy's voice at the beginning of the 1950s *Superman* TV series: "Faster than a speeding bullet. More powerful than a locomotive."

Bill Kennedy

Bill Kennedy

- Male and Female Since Adam and Eve (1961) ... Adam
- Bill Kennedy at the Movies (1959) TV Series
- I Died a Thousand Times (1955) ... Sheriff
- Unchained (1955) (uncredited)
- Loose in London (1953) (uncredited) ... Ship's Officer
- Red Planet Mars (1952) (uncredited) ... First News Commentator
- Nevada Badmen (1951) ... Jensen
- Canyon Raiders (1951) ... Hemingway (card sharp)
- Silver City Bonanza (1951) ... Monk Monroe
- Cry Danger (1951) (uncredited) ... Cop at Trailer Park
- Abilene Trail (1951) ... Colter
- Two Lost Worlds (1951) ... Martin Shannon
- Marshal of Trail City, The (1950) (TV)
- Border Outlaws (1950) ... Mr. Carson, guest
  ... aka Phantom Horseman, The (1950) (UK)
- Border Rangers (1950) ... Sergeant Carlson
- Train to Tombstone (1950) (uncredited) ... Jared Greeley, the Minister
- I Shot Billy the Kid (1950) ... Deputy Poe
- Peggy (1950) (uncredited) ... Reporter
- Storm Over Wyoming (1950) ... Jess Rawlins
- Gunslingers (1950) ... Ace Larabee
- Trail of the Yukon (1949) ... Constable
- Forgotten Women (1949) ... Bill Dunning
- Law of the West (1949) ... Dan Nixon
- Shadows of the West (1949) ... Jonathan Ward
- Assigned to Danger (1948) (as William Kennedy)

- In This Corner (1948) ... Al Barton, ring announcer
- Belle Starr's Daughter (1948) (uncredited) ... Kiowa Marshal
- Joan of Arc (1948) ... Thierache, her Executioner
- Sheriff of Medicine Bow (1948) ... Barry Stuart
- Southern Yankee, A (1948) (uncredited) ... Lt. Sheve
  ... aka My Hero (1948) (UK)
- Triggerman (1948) ... Kirby
- I Wouldn't Be in Your Shoes (1948) ... 2nd Detective
- Overland Trails (1948) ... Carter Morgan
- Gangster, The (1947) (uncredited) ... Thug
  ... aka Low Company (1951) (USA: reissue title)
- News Hounds (1947) ... Mark Morgan
- Case of the Baby-Sitter, The (1947) ... Homicide Lt. MacGruder
- Web of Danger (1947) ... Ernie Reardon
- Fun on a Weekend (1947) ... Bill Davis
- That Brennan Girl (1946) ... Arthur, Helen's Husband
- Bachelor's Daughters, The (1946) ... Mr. Stapp
  ... aka Bachelor Girls (1946) (UK)
- Don't Gamble with Strangers (1946) ... Harry Arnold
- Royal Mounted Rides Again, The (1945) ... Cpl. J. Wayne Decker
- Rhapsody in Blue (1945) ... Herbert Stone
- Escape in the Desert (1945) ... Hank Albright
- People's Choice, The (1944)
- Crime by Night (1944) (uncredited)
  ... Hospital Attendant
- Doughgirls, The (1944) (uncredited)
  ... Guy who punches Drake
- Mr. Skeffington (1944) ... Thatcher
- Make Your Own Bed (1944)
  (uncredited) ... George, FBI Agent

Kennedy's retirement followed the classic Kennedy style. He lived in Palm Beach, Florida, not far from Donald Trump and actor Douglas Fairbanks. He'd send wonderfully chatty, handwritten letters to friends. He died in Palm Beach at age 88.

## Liepchen (d: 1975)

This was Detroit's celebrity dog during the 1960s. The red miniature dachshund belonged to Mary Morgan, who hosted film and fashion programs on Channel 9. "Nobody pays attention to me," Morgan once told *Detroit News* television writer Frank Judge. "It's then I realize who the star of the show really is."

Morgan bought the 11-week-old pup in 1958 in Moscow, Michigan, as a pet. The dog's debut was quite accidental: Morgan put the dog on a sofa before introducing a film, and forgot about the animal. Viewers called, and then the dog became part of the show. It remained Detroit's top show-biz dog until Morgan retired in 1971. Liepchen died four years later.

## McBride, Jean

McBride hosted Detroit's first television cooking show, serving up three recipes daily between 1947 and 1960. *Detroit Free Press* feature writer Myra MacPherson described her in a 1959 profile as "that blue-eyed neighbor who's an expert on things like the kitchen and hooking rugs."

Miss McBride, as she was known, could have traded places with travelmeister George Pierrot. Before settling down at *The Detroit News* in 1936, she'd done quite a lot: taught school in Hawaii, Puerto Rico and the Philippine Islands; wrote ad copy in Los Angeles, and worked as a school principal in Mexico. She returned to her native Michigan (she was born in Burton) and got a job at the *News* as the newspaper's home economist. As she told the *Free Press'* MacPherson: "...when someone tells me how horrible anyplace is, I don't take his word for it. I go on my own. Anything new is bound to be interesting. I detest monotony, ruts. If I'm bored, it's my fault. If there's something lacking, it's up to me to fill the hole."

The attitude made her a perfect candidate for the new medium of television, starting a new Channel 4 career at age 46—an independent woman before her time.

## McCarthy, J.P. (d: 1995)

Why did basketball ace Michael Jordan yearn for a career in baseball? Maybe the answer to that would explain J.P. McCarthy's desire for a TV job.

McCarthy was the Michael Jordan of Detroit radio. His ratings were unfailingly high and he was paid accordingly. His command of the radio craft was unparalleled. Detroit's powerbrokers stumbled over themselves to cadge an invite to McCarthy's annual St. Patrick's Day party.

But McCarthy tried television, too. And just as Michael Jordan never made it out of the minor leagues, McCarthy never made much of an impact in TV. He had his own show on Channel 2 starting in 1983, but it was put to sleep in 1986. At one point, ABC brass thought about giving McCarthy a shot at hosting *Good Morning, America* but chose Charlie Gibson, instead. The last TV job McCarthy had was as host of Channel 50's specials on the North American International Auto Show from 1991 to 1995—nowhere near the success that McCarthy was accustomed to on radio. "This surely frustrated him," wrote McCarthy's former producer, Michael Shiels, in McCarthy's biography, *J.P. McCarthy: Just Don't Tell 'Em Where I Am.* Further, Shiels quotes former ABC official Dan Burke as saying that McCarthy's "primary goal was to get on television."

## Mann, Cathie

She and Bill Ratliff hosted Channel 4's *This Morning With Cathie Mann and Bill Ratliff* during the late 1970s. Mann was the

Detroit radio icon J.P. McCarthy tried his hand at television.

Channel 4's Cathie Mann later married "Gopher" from *The Love Boat.*

45

classic local-girl-makes-good-and-comes-home story. A graduate of Redford's Thurston High School and Michigan State University, she anchored newscasts in Los Angeles and Minneapolis before joining Channel 4 in 1977. Mann lasted two years at the station, becoming yet another old story: new-talk-show-host-hits-town-and-gets-crushed-in-ratings-war.

After leaving Channel 4, Mann wrote several potboilers (*Capitol Hill, Rumors, Tinsel Town*) and married Fred Grandy, who played Gopher on *The Love Boat*.

## Maxwell, Bob (d: 2001)

Most people assume that MTV invented music videos. Not true. Television viewers during the early 1950s watched Snader Telescriptions—visual renderings of songs by the popular songsters of the day. Now, we have hip-hop stars cavorting about to their own music. Back then, it was Nat King Cole, who did little cavorting but sang and played elegantly. Maxwell hosted *Man About Town*, during which he'd smoke cigarettes and explain the music to viewers. That made him Detroit's first veejay.

Maxwell started out in radio at WEXL-AM, where he was hired by Kirk Knight. Maxwell broke the news of Pearl Harbor to radio listeners in 1941. He later moved to Saginaw, but the story of his return is an honest-to-goodness fish tale. Edwin Wheeler, who ran the Evening News Association's broadcasting properties, heard Maxwell while on a fishing trip in Saginaw. Maxwell's strength was a pleasant, reassuring voice and urbane style. Initially hired to host WWJ-AM's morning show, Maxwell moved into the new medium of television during the late 1940s. He continued with various television host chores until leaving for CBS in 1961. Most of his later career involved "voice over" work. Maxwell reportedly made a fortune before retiring to southern California, where he lived until his death in 2001.

Bob Maxwell, Detroit's first "veejay."

## Melrose, Edythe Fern (d: 1976)

She was Detroit's Martha Stewart, before Martha Stewart invented the concept of Martha Stewart. Melrose was *The Lady of Charm* on WXYZ radio from 1941 to 1948, and then on Channel 7 from 1948 to 1960. The daily TV show set the standard for Detroit-area June Cleaver wannabees. "A woman's charm depends upon three things—how she acts, how she looks, how she cooks," was how Melrose once described her philosophy. And, like Stewart, Melrose was a flinty-eyed businesswoman who reaped a fortune. According to Dick Osgood's *W\*Y\*X\*I\*E Wonderland*, an authoritative history of Channel 7 and WXYZ-Radio, Melrose pulled in $100,000 from the two stations in 1952. That's $707,000 in 2004 dollars.

Melrose learned her style from Chicago's Bush Conservatory, where she studied to become an actress. As she told a *Detroit News* reporter in 1945, her education was based "upon the necessity of developing personality and charm—otherwise, he (her teacher and mentor, Elias Day) told us, people wouldn't tolerate us on the stage." Ever resourceful, Melrose carried what she learned to a radio station in Cleveland, teaching other women how to improve their surroundings. All along, Melrose conducted an awesome business career. Her gentle charm masked a business mind that would have intimidated Bill Gates. During the 1930s, when women were mostly restricted to secretarial work or education, Melrose managed a Cleveland radio station. When she came to Detroit later in the decade, it was to manage WJLB-AM.

By the time she got behind a microphone again at WXYZ and throughout her 20-year career, she combined business acumen and acting skills. Advertisers loved Melrose because she sold well to women. Station managers loved her because she made them tons of money. So persuasive was she that she had three "Houses O' Charm" during her tenure at Channel 7—wildly stylish and expensive homes from which she did her show.

Edythe Fern Melrose, The Lady of Charm.

*Auction Movie* host Fred Merle.

Her Detroit TV career lasted until 1960. While visiting the station eight years later to film a commercial, she tripped on a prop at Broadcast House and injured her leg. An Oakland County jury awarded her nearly $1 million in 1976, but she died three weeks later.

## Merle, Fred

Merle was among Channel 62's most recognizable faces, in addition to working as a producer/director on several ethnic television shows. Merle is best known for his dozen years (1978-1990) hosting *Auction Movie*, which aired variously on Thursday nights, Saturday mornings, Saturday afternoons and Monday nights. He had been working as a director at WGPR-TV when he approached Dr. William V. Banks, the station's founder, about going on the air. Banks' answer: "Merle, when do you want to start?"

Fred Merle grew up in Wyoming, and learned radio at Armed Forces Radio in Italy. He moved to Detroit in 1971, doing local news on WXON-TV. Not long after joining WGPR-TV as a free-lance director, he took control of *The Scene*, the station's trademark dance program. He also directed and/or produced ethnic programs focusing on the Yugoslav, Latino, Polish, Arabic and Greek communities. When his work at *Auction Movie* ran its course, he worked as the production manager for the Fox affiliate in Flint. Merle used his video skills to produce political commercials for several court candidates. More recently, he worked as a communications specialist for the city of Warren.

## Michigan Outdoors

*Michigan Outdoors* was Detroit television's biggest outdoors television show, which first aired in 1951.

*Michigan Outdoors* made a statewide TV star out of Mort Neff—who was not slated to be the original host. *Outdoor Life* correspondent Charlie East was supposed to host, with Neff as producer. But the *Outdoor Life* editors, paranoid about the new medium of television, nixed the idea of East hosting. So Neff took over—and stayed for decades.

Neff retired and sold the show to Jerry Chiappetta. The price: $50,000, payable at $10,000 per year. Chiappetta had it, but let it lapse—when it fell into Fred Trost's hands. It would have been there forever had Trost not been clobbered in a libel suit by a deer lure manufacturer, forcing both Trost and his production company into bankruptcy.

Channel 9's Mary Morgan.

## Morgan, Mary (d: 1989)

She was among Detroit's pioneer female broadcasters, and hosted *Million Dollar Movie* weekdays on Channel 9, often with her dog, Liepchen (d: 1975).

Elegant and refined, she did not lack self-esteem. She described herself as: "One of the most beautiful women in radio. It is therefore fitting that she should be Fashion and Beauty Editor of CKLW for she indeed fits her role in every detail, being the very expression of charm, beauty and example of the very latest fashion trends of which she speaks…"

Like most television pioneers, Morgan started in radio. She grew up in Hamilton, Ontario, joining WWJ-AM during the early 1930s. She moved her act across the Detroit River to CKLW-AM a few years later, then branched into television during the 1950s. Until her 1971 retirement, she remained the embodiment of a fashionable movie hostess. After her retirement, she lived in an apartment on the Detroit side of the Detroit River.

## Murphy, Bob

"The Tall Boy in the Third Row," as Murphy was known, was 6 feet 8 inches tall and one of the busiest men in Detroit show business. In addition to working as a deejay on WJBK-AM during the 1950s, he was a big presence on Channel 2, where he hosted *Ladies' Day*, *Breakfast with Murphy* and *The Morning Show*. Each of the chat programs included celebrity interviews. And it earned him big money for the day—$40,000-$50,000 a year. He even got a bit part on *Gunsmoke*, with a dozen lines of dialogue for which he was paid $100.

After graduating from the University of Toledo and working in Ohio radio, Murphy joined WJBK-AM in 1948. One of the hottest broadcast outlets in town, the station also boasted a show by "Jack the Bellboy," a.k.a. Ed McKenzie. Since everybody had a fancy show-biz handle, Murphy had to have one. He chose "The Tall Boy in the Third Row," a nickname he came to hate. When television became big in the 1950s, he joined on.

After a dozen years on Detroit television, Murphy chucked it all in 1967. "I wasn't sure what I wanted, but I had a profound conviction about what I didn't want," he later told *The Detroit News'* Art O'Shea. "Being a television personality pays well, but it's shallow work and very boring." Murphy later went into advertising.

## Neff, Mort (d: 1990)

Michigan has the best and most varied hunting and fishing of perhaps any state in the union, and Mort Neff brought it to southeast Michigan television viewers with *Michigan Outdoors*. A Birmingham native and 1927 graduate of the University of Michigan, Neff had a diverse career before ranging around Michigan full-time. He worked as a tennis pro in Monte Carlo and a radio operator for an Arctic expedition. He also distinguished himself as a producer. When ad man Fran Congdon dreamed up *Michigan Outdoors*, Neff had a new job.

*Michigan Outdoors* bounced between Channels 4 and 7. Neff's program was an honest, unadulterated, exuberant celebration of the state's outdoor life. Lower Michiganians who headed north in search of fish and game appreciated Neff's efforts. His compass pointed south, too. He once traveled to Chile in search of trout. And

Mort Neff celebrated Michigan's outdoors.

none of this was an act. If Neff was fond of a particular stagehand, he'd bestow them with a string tie anchored by a Petoskey stone.

Neff retired in 1973 and turned *Michigan Outdoors* over to Jerry Chiappetta and Fred Trost, although the line of succession becomes a bit fuzzy. Neff lived for another 17 years, dying in northern Michigan in 1990, at age 86. He is buried in Emmet County, Friendship Township.

## Orlando, Tony

Singer Tony Orlando made a stab at a syndicated television show in the 1980s from Channel 4's downtown Detroit studios. Orlando had been one of the top recording artists of the 1970s, with "Knock Three Times" (1971) and "Tie A Yellow Ribbon 'Round the Ole Oak Tree" (1973). His career went even further with a CBS variety program from 1974 to 1976.

He could talk. He could sing. He could tell jokes. So King World Productions, the company that gave us *Oprah, Wheel of Fortune* and *Jeopardy!* took a chance at testing a syndicated show from Detroit. Channel 4, which had ties to King World, was chosen as ground zero for the experiment.

Orlando's program lasted six weeks. He now lives and performs in Branson, Missouri. Somehow, Orlando forgot to mention Detroit in his autobiography.

## Osgood, Dick (d: 2000)

It was Osgood's voice that literally launched Channel 7 when it went on the air October 9, 1948. He later hosted television movies and *Starlit Stairway,* and also did movie reviews. However, he was known more for his radio work than his TV work.

He wrote what is easily the best memoir about Detroit broadcasting—a very short list, of course: *W\*Y\*X\*I\*E Wonderland* is an accounting of who Osgood knew, and he knew everybody. He knew Bill Bonds as a rookie TV newscaster and Dick Purtan as a

Conrad Patrick, star of TV and radio.

George Pierrot toured 117 countries.

rookie WKNR-AM deejay. Osgood, the last of the gentlemen in broadcasting, was nice to everybody on their way up. When they got to the top, they remembered him fondly.

When Osgood showed up at Channel 7's 50th anniversary party, he was a hit. He appeared on the same stage with Soupy Sales, Bill Bonds, Marilyn Turner and John Kelly, but was not upstaged. Although it was a black-tie affair, Osgood nevertheless looked elegant in a turtleneck sweater and a suit jacket. "I gave my tux to the bartender," he said in a speech.

### Patrick, Conrad (d: 1988)

Patrick worked at various jobs at Channel 9, but was known mostly as Bill Kennedy's vacation replacement on *Showtime*. Patrick later became Kennedy's permanent replacement on Channel 9 when Kennedy moved to Channel 50 in 1969.

Highly successful as a radio host, Patrick worked at numerous Detroit radio stations—including CKLW, WKNR (now WNIC), WJBK and WCAR. During the late 1960s, he held several posts at Channel 9. In addition to subbing for Kennedy, Patrick anchored the news and worked as the station's staff announcer. Many Detroit viewers remember him best as the man who sat next to Mr. Belvedere (real name: Maurice Lezell) on Belvedere's commercials. The standard cut to the Belvedere spot: "I'm glad you asked me that, Conrad."

### Pierrot, George (d: 1980)

George Pierrot was the longest running and perhaps most successful host in Detroit television history. And he did it by showing peoples' vacation movies. His first television appearance occurred on Channel 7 on October 10, 1948, the station's second day in business. Pierrot later moved to Channel 4, where his afternoon travel show aired from 1949 until 1976. At his 80th birthday bash at the Detroit Institute of Arts in 1978, 2,000 guests

**A typical week on George Pierrot's show might embrace three or four continents. Here's Christmas week, 1964.**

**December 21, 1964, 5 p.m.:**
Arthur M. Dewey, Cleveland world traveler and naturalist, presents "The Wonders of Chile."

**December 21, 1964, 7 p.m.:**
Dewey: "Tahiti—Gem of the South Seas."

**December 22, 1964:**
Dewey: "Holiday in Chile." Christmas Day in the little mining town of Andecolla.

**December 23, 1964:**
Dewey: "Scandinavian Holiday."

**December 24, 1964:**
Dewey: "6,000 Miles Through Turkey."

**December 25, 1964:**
Dewey: "Turkey Today."

*Source: George F. Pierrot papers, Burton Historical Collection.*

helped him blow out the candles. He also hosted the DIA's "World Adventure" film-and-lecture series for 46 years, from 1933 until 1979.

Pierrot makes no sense as a television star, unless one thinks about the early history of the medium. His voice was gravely, his hair was thin and his girth proved his love of international cuisine. However, he had two things that sold him to his vast audience. One was credibility. "If he asked a question of a guest who'd been in some obscure country, chances are George had already been there twice," recalls Seymour Kapetansky, a friend. The other was the most valuable commodity of all in the early days of television: exciting pictures. In a medium that was forced to show fish tanks because it had nothing else to show, this made Pierrot valuable, indeed.

Pierrot was born January 11, 1898. The son of a physician, Pierrot grew up in suburban Seattle, Washington. As he wrote in his papers, which can be found in Detroit's Burton Historical Collection: "This was frontier country—young men's country— raw, boisterous, surging with energy and optimism." As a student at the University of Washington, he made money doing various things—longshoring and canning salmon in Alaska, and by covering the campus for the *Seattle Times.* His early life in a pre-broadcast era resembled the way people lived for centuries. Detailing his high school years working in his family's apple orchard, he wrote: "My daily routine, for four summers, was to rise at six, take a plunge in an irrigation ditch, breakfast hastily, and rent a team, with which I cultivated the soil between the trees from seven to six."

Pierrot arrived in Detroit as an editor of *The American Boy— Youth's Companion Magazine,* a national publication based in Detroit. Founded in 1899, the magazine entertained young males with exciting stories in the days long before computer games and TV wrestling. He edited the magazine for a dozen years, until 1936. Pierrot's entry into the world of video was something of a fluke, but his preoccupation with traveling was not. Given a 100-day leave of absence from *American Boy* in 1931, he took off on a dash around the world with stops in China and Japan. Pierrot spun it into a book in 1935, *The Vagabond Trail,* a vivid description of the Far East in the days before World War II. Only two years after that trip, he founded the DIA's "World Adventure Series." The Depression almost took the DIA down the financial chute, but Pierrot began hosting Sunday afternoon events in which a world traveler would show up with footage and talk about his (or her) trip. It saved the cash-starved DIA during tough times, and was so successful that Pierrot quit *American Boy* in 1936 to work full time on the series.

It made sense when Channel 7 came calling a dozen years later. He had pictures from all over the world. Channel 7 convinced Pierrot that television would be good publicity. "World Adventure Series" went on to become the oldest adventure/travel program on TV. *George Pierrot Presents*, which debuted on Channel 4 on February 19, 1953, became one of the station's franchise shows. Channel 4 could not get enough of his work, running the show seven times per week. (The show also aired Sundays on Channel 7 at the same time it ran weekdays on Channel 4.) The show regularly numbered among the top five Detroit-based programs on the air. Highlights included an eagle named Mr. Ramshaw eating a raw turkey head and a skunk biting Pierrot until he bled.

It was nothing more than Pierrot sitting there, asking questions of the guest who came bearing film from far off lands. But something about Pierrot—maybe his earnestness, maybe his knowledge—made him an attractive host. He looked like somebody's uncle who'd been everywhere, seen everything. Off camera, Pierrot was a legend, a regular at the Detroit Press Club, where he'd hold court telling dirty limericks. "Adventure is within rather than without you," he said. "It is a state of mind. Two men can take the same walk. One will come back brimful of stories about interesting and amazing incidents he witnessed. The other will return bored. He has seen nothing, heard nothing." Pierott's TV career ended in 1976.

He was fond of quoting St. Augustine (d: 430), who said: "The world is a book, of which they who never stir from home read but a page." His obituaries in 1980 noted he toured 117 countries.

Pierrot's last words as the ambulance drivers took him on his final trip: "One of you boys better drive. I don't feel up to it."

*Profiles In Black* host Dr. Gil Maddox.

## Profiles In Black

Hosted by Dr. Gil Maddox, this weekly public affairs program aired on Channel 4 and featured interviews with some of Detroit's most prominent African-Americans of the late 1960s and 1970s. Some of Maddox's guests included Motown's Supremes and Smokey Robinson, sports figures such as basketball's Bill Russell, most members of the Detroit City Council and, on several occasions, Detroit Mayor Coleman A. Young. Two U.S. senators (Donald Riegle and Carl Levin) also made appearances on the program, which aired during prime time or early evenings on Saturdays, Sundays or Mondays between 1969 and 1981.

Maddox knew whereof he spoke. A graduate of Northern High School, he was advised as a youth that he ought to explore manual labor as a potential livelihood. Because of that—or perhaps in spite of that—Maddox went on to earn a Ph.D. in communications from Wayne State University and taught at several Michigan universities during his TV tenure. He also worked at Detroit's Focus:HOPE.

Maddox later joined a team that bid unsuccessfully for the City of Detroit's cable television franchise. He now lives in semi-retirement in Washington, D.C.

## Purtan, Dick

Radio host Dick Purtan's career has been one of the most successful ever in Detroit. He tried television—once.

Purtan starred in a one-hour comedy special December 2, 1981, on Channel 4. The show was a colossal success, and pulled roughly 45 percent of the local TV audience that night and won a 1981 Emmy as Best Entertainment Show.

But Purtan, the Zen master of the radio medium, didn't care much for the process of making television. "After watching that hour, I sat there and said to myself, 'We worked for three months on this. And, poof, it's gone after an hour.'" He never did another show.

## Scott, Agnes (d: 1997)

She was the face, the brains and the soul behind Channel 56's fund-raising auction. Annoying though it may be, the auction made millions for the public TV station. It's one of the reasons Channel 56 morphed from a small-budget educational video service in the 1960s into the reasonably decent broadcaster it became in the 1970s. She also coordinated the hundreds of volunteers who worked for the station during the auction, serving as Channel 56's public face to public TV's biggest fans.

Scott was there at the station's debut auction, serving as chairperson for the first event in 1969. Within a year, she became the auction manager and volunteer director; then moved up to become the station's development director (read: chief fundraiser) until 1984. At the time of her death in 1997, she was Channel 56's vice president of special projects.

## Slagle, Johnny (d: 1967)

He was among local television's first stars. Slagle appeared on Channel 7 during the early 1950s, first in *Johnny In the Afternoon*, and later with the *Pat 'n' Johnny Show*—which starred Slagle and hostess Pat Tobin—a forerunner of the modern-day Regis Philbin morning talk program. Since television hadn't existed and the TV talk show genre hadn't been created, Slagle, Tobin and their producers were forced to devise ways to fill time. Tobin and Slagle would chat about their weekend activities, last night's dinner—whatever struck their interest. Celebrities would stop by. Pets would gad about. Mostly ad-lib, it would run for as long as three hours. The word broadcast historian Dick Osgood used often when describing Slagle was

Johnny Slagle, Detroit's first TV star.

"jolly." When Pat and Johnny ran out of things to say, the camera would focus on an aquarium while somebody thought of something else to do or say. "We didn't know what else to do," said Mort Zieve, a Channel 7 director from the era.

After *Pat 'n' Johnny* folded in the early 1950s, Slagle split his time between WXYZ-radio and television. He hosted *River Boat Jazz* on radio, and announced *Motor City Wrestling*. By the mid-1960s, he was out of show business entirely.

Slagle, who died in 1967, spent the last two years of his life selling boats at the Jefferson Beach Marina.

## Tobin, Pat

She was Detroit's first female television star. Tobin and Johnny Slagle hosted *The Pat 'n' Johnny Show*, which aired weekday afternoons on Channel 7. Tobin and her partner would talk, play records and interview celebrities. Since the ABC Network had barely developed and the television business was in its infancy, the duo would simply talk and sing until they ran out of things to talk about and music to play. Then, they would return to the air when they figured out their next move. "Nobody cared if it was timed to the second because nobody had seen television before," recalls Ron David, a veteran Channel 7 producer. "The trick was getting it on the air."

Tobin and Slagle did the show out of Channel 7's Studio 15D, atop the Maccabees Building. "It was about the size of a kitchen," recalls David. The commercials were live.

The show went off the air in 1951, after which Tobin left town. Slagle returned to WXYZ-radio, and later hosted a Channel 7 wrestling show.

## Trost, Fred

Trost currently hosts *Practical Sportsman*, the second generation of *Michigan Outdoors*. Most outside observers think that

Pat Tobin teamed with Johnny Slagle to host Detroit's first talk/variety show.

would make Trost the television heir to the legacy of Mort Neff, with whom Trost had a close association for years. But plenty of people boast a Neff connection. Maybe, someday, a Ph.D. candidate will do a dissertation sorting out who Mort Neff's true heir is. But, for now, Trost will have to do.

Trost and Neff first met in 1968, just before Trost's graduation from Michigan State University with majors in English and natural resources. Neff was getting on in years, and was looking for a successor to continue the *Michigan Outdoors* legacy. Trost's qualifications—especially the college major in natural resources—seemed like an appropriate fit. A mutual friend introduced the two, and Trost cooked up an audition tape—something featuring a fake rabbit and Trost's wife. Neff liked the idea and loaned Trost a camera for further work. Trost subsequently made 112 appearances on *Michigan Outdoors* during the next three years.

Trost left *Michigan Outdoors* in 1971 to try his hand at documentary production. Later, he created *Michigan Weekend*—a kind of *Michigan Outdoors,* but with a female perspective supplied by his first wife. That didn't work. "We had a travel segment and a cooking segment, along with an outdoor segment. We wanted a show with broad appeal, but the show was just too broad. The hunters out there didn't want to watch a sissy segment on travel," Trost said.

At the same time, the TV industry began to change. "Strip" shows were introduced to the airwaves—meaning game shows and reruns that could be run the same time every night of the week. That drove shows like Trost's—which aired only once a week—right off the air.

It was at that time that *Michigan Outdoors* fell to Trost. After Jerry Chiappetta left the show, Trost inherited it and hosted the program between 1981 and 1992. Trost ran into legal trouble (the non-criminal type) during the 1990s. Trost told TV viewers that a certain deer scent wasn't really deer urine, but cow urine.

The company objected strenuously, and a Montcalm County jury awarded the firm $4 million. The award put Trost out of business, although he recovered and resurrected himself with *Practical Sportsman.*

The concept of *Practical Sportsman* on public television is actually funny. "I'd have a guy on who'd say something like, 'I seen a deer running through the woods'—just torturing the language. But people loved it," Trost said. They still do. *Practical Sportsman* is still a big draw for public television stations at pledge time.

## Watkins, R.J.

Watkins was a Detroit version of Johnny Carson or Aaron Spelling—a TV host who also dreamed up and produced shows. He was one of Channel 62's best-known personalities before the station was sold to CBS, and was the brains behind many of the station's high-profile programs. Watkins hosted *Late Night Entertainment*, an interview/variety show that aired weekends; often hosted *The Scene*, which was maybe the hippest dance show ever to hit Detroit television; and produced numerous specials, such as Channel 62's New Year's Eve extravaganza.

To Watkins, Detroit wasn't a TV "market." It was home. He moved from Macon, Georgia, when he was 3 years old. His father started out as a mechanic, eventually working his way up to become the first black Standard Oil franchisee in Detroit. Watkins' father later bought a party store, and lost his life in a holdup there.

The younger Watkins never had much interest in the liquor or gasoline businesses. Show business interested him. A graduate of Pershing High School, Watkins was awarded a dance scholarship but quickly bailed out. "But I did learn how to count," he recalls.

One of his early video ventures featured a production with The Floaters, who had a hit, "Float On." Watkins shot the group, appropriately enough, floating on the Detroit River. (The video was shot by Rick Lassiter and Nat Morris, who was already a star as host of *The Scene*.) "I didn't know what I was doing," Watkins remembered, "but it was great." Later, Watkins worked for Morris at *The Scene*, and gravitated to his own show on Channel 62, *Late Night Entertainment*, an interview/variety program that featured interviews with everybody from Vanessa Williams to The Temptations. The show lasted from 1981 until 1995. After that, Watkins went on to own his own low-power radio and television station.

## Watts, John D. (d: 1965)

Before *Judge Judy* and *Court TV* there was Judge John Watts, the real-life judge who ruled on Channel 4's *Traffic Court* during the 1950s. The show, shot in Channel 4's downtown Detroit studios, featured actors who recreated real-life cases. Devised by Channel 4 producers Seymour Kapetansky and Vic Hurwitz, actors would read a court transcript for the case being "tried," then ad-lib dialogue when the cameras went on. The show was thought to be a first in the country.

The star of the show, Judge Watts, was among Detroit's most famous citizens. A native Detroiter, Watts graduated from Detroit's Central High School and the Detroit College of Law. He was elected to the Common Pleas court in 1931, and then appointed to Detroit's Traffic Court in 1945. Watts was noted for his special contempt of drunk drivers and slumlords.

Watts thought *Traffic Court* served an educational purpose. However, the state Bar of Michigan in 1957 deemed the show an advertisement and called a halt to Watts' involvement. He last appeared on *Traffic Court* on September 24, 1957.

## Wholey, Dennis

Wholey hosted what may be the only nightly network television show ever to originate in Detroit: *PBS LateNight* (later titled *LateNight with Dennis Wholey*) aired weeknights from Channel

*Traffic Court's* John D. Watts.

56's New Center studios between 1982 and 1984. As television interview shows became more frantic and confrontational, Wholey went in the opposite direction. His interviews were noted for their calm. Wholey, usually casually clad in a sweater, conversed quietly with his guest of the evening and took calls from viewers.

He started out as a tour guide at NBC in New York City. As described in Wholey's book, *The Courage To Change* (1984), Wholey began drinking more as he moved further up the broadcasting food chain from tour guide to radio director to FM radio interviewer. "I'm told that one night in a bar I told Edward Albee how to write plays," he recalled in his book. After breaking in as a talk show host in Cincinnati, Wholey was invited to Detroit for a weeklong tryout at Channel 7. He stayed for four years.

As related by Wholey, sobering up enabled him to work at probably his biggest success—*PBS LateNight*. *The Courage To Change*, a collection of interviews with both famous and not-so-famous alcoholics, put him on *The New York Times* best-seller list. More recently, he has hosted a nationally syndicated talk show from Washington, D.C.

## Wolf, Fred (d: 2000)

He was huge, both on television and radio. Wolf's *Wacky Wigloo* program was heard on WXYZ-AM between 1950 and 1965, after which Wolf's aversion to playing rock 'n' roll records guaranteed his exit from the medium. He was also a seminal influence at Channel 7, where Wolf anchored a long list of sporting activities normally associated with blue collar sports fans—of which, of course, there were (and are) many in Detroit. Wolf's specialties included bowling, boat racing, hot rodding and wrestling. At one point, Wolf's *Championship Bowling* was seen on some 150 stations across the country. In Detroit, it was a must-see for bowlers when it aired on Channel 7 Sundays at noon. In the end, he managed something few others have ever

Dennis Wholey conducted calm interviews.

dared: He became the only morning deejay to also pull off a successful television career. The late J.P. McCarthy tried, but failed. Dick Purtan had little interest in TV. But Wolf managed to combine both.

If Wolf appealed to blue collar Detroit, it was because he was one of them. One of the problems with contemporary local broadcasting is that its on-air talent has lost its connection with the town. The university broadcasting schools turn out generic "talent" acceptable to Omaha, or Atlanta or Detroit. Most broadcasters refer to Detroit (or any other big U.S. city) as a "market." Wolf was the exact opposite. He never went to broadcast school.

What Fred Wolf knew about Detroit, he learned—literally—from inside a factory or a bowling alley. As a young man, Wolf worked at the Chrysler plant that made Sherman tanks during World War II. When he wasn't building instruments of destruction, Wolf was bowling. He earned a spot on the Stroh Brewing Co. bowling team (back problems forced him off the lanes and into the job of team manager). His experience in the alleys gave him credibility when he produced a pilot episode of a bowling show for radio. He was leery about getting into a business he knew nothing about, but a WJR executive talked him into the broadcasting project, and several advertisers further encouraged Wolf to develop the show. Bowling-crazy Detroit loved it. *Talking Ten Pins* lasted roughly six months on the radio. More important, it proved to be a marvelous calling card for Channel 7 boss John Pival, who was an expert at spotting raw talent. He spotted it with Soupy Sales, with Rita Bell, with Dave Diles and with Bill Bonds. And he spotted it with Wolf.

Wolf was seen everywhere. And he spoke to viewers in a language they understood. If radio could be split into "pre-Beatles" and "post-Beatles" eras, so could television. Wolf was the best TV had to offer in the pre-Beatles era.

Fred Wolf in his natural habitat—a Detroit-area bowling alley.

# Horror

*Every town had its own collection of horror hosts during the 1950s and 1960s. It was its own art form. And just as art has its different sorts of schools, so did Detroit's horror hosts. The Ghoul's act approached nihilism. If you took away the makeup, Sir Graves Ghastly's act would have worked in vaudeville. Here are the people who scared the pants off Detroit kids in years past.*

## Ghastly, Sir Graves

Sir Graves (real name: Lawson Deming) amused kids with his Saturday afternoon horror movie show, which he hosted from 1966 through 1983. In addition to playing a vampire with a fiendish laugh and intense stare, he played a prodigiously varied cast of characters who gave the show a unique sense of style and pacing.

A native of Cleveland, Deming started out in Detroit as a puppeteer for *Woodrow the Woodsman*, a Channel 2 children's show host who was seen here during the early and mid-1960s. But Woodrow liked Cleveland (whence he came) better than Detroit, and decided to return. Deming stayed and created Sir Graves. At one point during the late 1960s, Sir Graves' show was the most

Sir Graves was a Saturday afternoon fixture.

popular offering on Saturday afternoon Detroit TV.

Deming was less edgy than *The Ghoul,* but no less creative. His cast of characters included The Glob, Baruba, Baron Boofaloff, Tilly Trollhouse (That Gorgeous Cookie) and the Reel McCoys—twin grave diggers who dug up the movie for the day. And, of course, Sir Graves would crawl in and out of his coffin before speaking. "I don't really remember scaring anyone in particular," he once told writer Christopher Walton in a *Detroit Free Press* interview.

As of the writing of this book, Deming is happily retired, in his early 90s, and living with his wife of more than 60 years. His son, David, who studied at Cranbrook, is president of the Cleveland Institute of Art.

## Ghoul, The

He was a floating miasma of mayhem who appeared on late night Detroit television during the 1970s and 1980s. The Ghoul (real name: Ron Sweed) hosted low-budget horror movies on Channel 50 between 1971 and 1975 and later on Channels 20 and 62. He lived in Waterford Township between 1975 and 1979. His monologues were punctuated with jokes about Parma, the Cleveland-area equivalent of Hamtramck.

The Ghoul's act may seem like a chaotic mess dreamed up at the spur of the moment, but The Ghoul has a philosophical lineage. Sweed was an ardent disciple of Cleveland's Ernie Anderson, who played *Ghoulardi* on Cleveland television. As Sweed explained in his autobiography, *The Ghoul: A Scrapbook* ($17.95, Gray & Company, Cleveland), Anderson himself bequeathed the Ghoul's fright wig, moustache and beard to Sweed, along with "Oxnard," a skull used as a prop on The Ghoul's set. Sweed outfitted Oxnard with a movable jaw "so he could Papa Ooo Mow Mow with the best of them."

Sweed broke into Cleveland television in 1971, was syndicat-

The Ghoul: Turn blue and scratch glass.

ed to Detroit's Channel 50 not long afterward, and remained on Detroit TV until the 1980s. What worked in Cleveland, which some regard as a Lake Erie version of Detroit, also worked in the Motor City. Sweed's shtick involved equal parts fireworks, Polish jokes and absurdist humor. Imagine a teenage boy's psyche sprung to life, and that's The Ghoul's show. "I'm on? Of course I am. I lit up a kielbasi just during the last movie segment. It took me places you never imagined, over-dey. You won't believe. We're on, huh?" would be a typical line.

Cleveland-area television critics Tom Feran and R.D. Heldenfels, writing in *Cleveland TV Memories*, made an exhaustive list of the items the The Ghoul blew up during his show: "Kielbasa, pizza, model cars, carp, Cheez Whiz, turkeys, soup cans, garbage cans, pierogies, toilets, film reels, LP records, shirts, viewer mail, guitars, model airplanes, Mickey Mouse, Beatle figurines, televisions, model boats, radios, skulls, arts and crafts, 45 rpm records, 5-quart containers of strawberries, flared pants, and the back of a fan's Levis." And that's not even mentioning the much-tortured "Froggy."

Although managers liked the revenue The Ghoul brought to a normally dead time period (Saturday nights), they didn't always appreciate his act. One station manager nixed the Ghoul's use of "homemade cannons, rockets, fire bombs, or other potentially dangerous items sent in by viewers (to) be demonstrated on the Ghoul show … the risk of injury in the studio or viewer imitation is too high." This would be like telling Eric Clapton to rid himself of two strings out of six on his guitar. On the brighter side, The Ghoul did have his defenders. One station manager wrote an angry viewer that: "The Ghoul's humor draws from the 'theater of the absurd,' a type of comedy that is generally absent from television today." The memo was written in 1972. It's even truer 30 years later. However, Sweed can still be seen in Cleveland. And at the time of this writing, he was plotting a Detroit comeback.

The Ghoul: "… do it while you can, but don't get caught."

Morgus the Magnificent.

By the way, this is how the Ghoul signed off his show:

"Well, I got enough time to make it to the bar for a couple of last rounds, over-dey, so home to Queen Barbara. Love you, baby. And until next week I want all of you out there to stay sick, turn blue, scratch glass, climb walls; but most importantly of all, do it while you can, but don't get caught. Bye!"

## Morgus the Magnificent

He was one of Detroit's favorite TV horror show hosts, although he wasn't strictly a Detroit product. Morgus (real name: Sid Noel, a.k.a. Sidney Noel Rideau) came from New Orleans. But when he brought *Morgus Presents* to Detroit in 1964, it became known as a made-in-Detroit product, and is still remembered that way, although he was only here for a few years.

Morgus (full name: Dr. Momus Alexander Morgus) created an entertaining and ornate fantasy world. He directed the Momus Alexander Morgus Institute, in the mythical city of Icehouse. His landlady (and manager) was Mrs. Fetish, and Morgus' more peculiar patients (or victims?) were located in a secret room. How did he get that handprint on the left side of his lab coat? One television scholar, the late Elena M. Watson, surmised that "this handprint, along with Morgus' perpetually stooped posture, is symbolic of life pushing him down." Morgus didn't carry the program by himself. There was Chopsley, a lumbering, bumbling helper. Morgus would tell Chopsley, "Some of us were born to serve, Chopsley, and some of us were born to command. It was Aristotle who said that—or was it I?" There was Eric, a skull that escaped Morgus' abuse through blatant obsequiousness.

*Morgus Presents* originally aired 11:30 p.m. Fridays, which presented a bit of a problem for Channel 2. Steve Allen had the time period, and wasn't all that happy about being displaced by a former rock disc jockey in a filthy lab coat. (The station solved the problem by giving viewers a 90-minute Allen rerun at 5:30

p.m. Saturdays.) Morgus was granted his own five-minute week-day weathercast on Channel 2, which was syndicated to stations in Milwaukee and Atlanta.

His success during the early 1960s, particularly in New Orleans, was astonishing. He starred in his own movie, *The Wacky World of Dr. Morgus* (1961), and once drew a crowd of 80,000 in New Orleans. The 1970s and 1980s weren't quite as good to Morgus. But he hasn't been forgotten—especially in Detroit.

## Scary, Count

A good-natured vampire, played by WOMC-FM's Tom Ryan. Channel 4 was looking for a host for a 3-D movie, *Gorilla At Large*, when producer Tom De Lisle, at the behest of program director Henry Maldonado, came up with the idea of Count Scary. The concept was borrowed, or stolen, from Canada's SCTV, which had a character by the name of Count Floyd. Count Floyd, played by Joe Flaherty, would let rip with the phrase, "Oooooh, that's scary." Hence, the birth of Count Scary, who was quoted as saying "imitation is the sincerest form of Flaherty."

Scary's gags were well-developed, and involved virtually everybody at the station. Ryan could be seen driving around town in his "Scarymobile," a pink, 1955 Chrysler Imperial that often fell apart between takes. During one skit, he interrupted Channel 4 editorial director Beth Konrad, who was about as serious as anybody in Detroit TV, and even popped in during a newscast. Often, he had help from his "fine, fine boys."

Ryan went on to play the Count in nine Channel 4 prime time specials, later taking the character to Channels 7 and 50.

Count Scary at The Palace of Auburn Hills.

# Wrestling

*They weren't pretty. They weren't subtle.*
*Often, they could barely talk. But they could certainly entertain.*
*Here are Detroit's foremost TV grapplers.*

### Brazil, Bobo (d: 1998)

Brazil (real name: Houston Harris) was famous for the "coco butt." As any fan could testify, that meant Brazil crashing his head against the head of an opponent. There was a lot of velocity behind the head: statistics peg Brazil at anywhere between 6 foot 4 inches and 6 foot 6 inches and somewhere around 270 pounds. He was known for two other things: breaking the color barrier in the grappling industry—where he is generally remembered as the "Jackie Robinson of Wrestling"—and for an ugly, longstanding feud with The Sheik, a rivalry that went on for four decades.

Born in Arkansas, he grew up in East St. Louis, Illinois, before moving to Benton Harbor as a youngster. In the early and mid-1960s, tickets with Brazil at New York City's Madison Square Garden could draw capacity crowds—and then some. The overbooked Garden turned away 5,000 fans away from a 1964 match,

Bobo Brazil was famous for the dishing out a dreaded "coco butt."

Dick the Bruiser in a good mood.

Leaping Larry Chene.

in which Brazil wrestled Hans "The Great" Mortier of Nuremberg, Germany.

A bit of wrestling trivia: Brazil lost one of his titles to "Nature Boy" Ric Flair in 1977, setting Flair's career into high gear. Brazil was still wrestling as late as 1990. He operated Bobo's Grill in Benton Harbor for two decades before his death in 1998. He's still memorialized in the southwestern Michigan town, where he died. Visitors can check in at the Bobo Brazil Community Center.

### Bruiser, Dick the (d: 1991)

Wrestling's blue-collar hero of the 1950s and 1960s, Bruiser was the surliest hombre ever to wear black trunks. There was nothing subtle about this man—which is the way the fans liked it: He drank beer, smoked cigars and communicated with an inarticulate crude growl that was to become his trademark. *The Ring Chronicle,* in its induction of Bruiser into The Professional Wrestling Hall of Fame, called him "the original, *real* toughest S.O.B. in pro wrestling."

Bruiser (real name: Richard Afflis) played offensive line with the Green Bay Packers (1951-1954) before becoming a wrestling star. Wrestling thrives on bad guys, and Bruiser fit the bill. He held dozens of titles during his day, either alone or with his favorite tag-team partner, The Crusher.

Bruiser and former Detroit Lion football star Alex Karras fought in one of Detroit's great brawls: a 1963 fracas that became barroom legend. Bruiser and Karras met at downtown Detroit's Lindell AC for lunch. They had agreed to an "impromptu" fight during lunch to publicize an upcoming wrestling match. Bruiser got a little carried away. An entire squad of Detroit cops was needed to break up the fight, which hit the pages of *The Detroit News* and *Free Press.* The ploy worked.

Bruiser died at age 62 from a heart attack at his winter home in Florida.

## Chene, Leaping Larry (d: 1964)

Leaping Larry Chene (real name: Arthur Lawrence Beauchene) thrilled youngsters during the 1950s and 1960s with his flying pirouettes in the wrestling ring. Chene played one of the good guys, somebody the fans could cheer for without feeling guilty. Bad guys such as Brute Bernard would do damage to Larry, but before they knew it they would be face-to-face with the bottoms of Larry's boots. To invert a current wrestling phrase: This was not a good thing. This was a bad thing.

Chene died in an automobile crash in Illinois in 1964, leaving Detroit wrestling fans in grief.

## Curry, Wild Bull (d: 1985)

Fred "Wild Bull" Curry (real name: Fred Khoury) looked like a man who missed the pleasures of human evolution. Consider the package: eyebrows joined in the middle, abundant body hair, gravel-tinged voice.

Curry grew up in Hartford, Connecticut, beginning his professional life as a cop. As he told *Hartford Courant* reporter J. Michael Kenyon in 1983: "I was getting $42 a week as a cop. I just couldn't make it on that." So Curry took up wrestling, although he never entirely abandoned law enforcement as a sideline.

Between the 1930s and early 1970s, Curry was the model of the untamed bad guy. "Where there was Bull, there was blood," said Hal Sullivan, a former ring announcer and CBC newsman. "If he were in with a young guy, a guy with no experience, Bull would try to damage him in some way that was unexpected. The most common injury when you'd wrestle Bull was a broken nose or broken teeth. He'd do that just so you'd know you'd been in the ring with Bull." The odd thing about Bull, according to Sullivan, was that "Bull was the same way outside the ring as inside."

Out of the ring, Curry would usually wear a tweed suit coat that was bagged at the elbows, a lumberjack shirt and old pants.

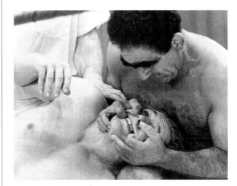

Curry: Part-time dental hygienist?

Ernie "The Cat" Ladd.

Channel 9's Lord Layton.

What people probably didn't realize is that they were looking at a millionaire—or at least rumored to be. He allegedly owned land in Hartford. In the years before his death, Curry worked as a cop in his native Hartford. Deputy Sheriff Bull Curry would escort prisoners between jail and Hartford Superior Court. He was good at it.

## Ladd, Ernie "The Cat"

Ladd was known as "The Big Cat," and for good reason. Ladd stood 6 feet 9 inches and weighed 320 pounds. In contrast to Dick the Bruiser, who seemed to revel in beer, cigars and pointedly unathletic activity, Ladd was a first-class athlete. He had been a football star with the San Diego Chargers (1961-1965), Houston Oilers (1966-67) and Kansas City Chiefs (1967-68), taking up wrestling during the off season. Big and unusually agile, he had one other shtick that gave him a certain show-biz cache: He liked to cheat.

One of Ladd's biggest moments occurred in Detroit in February 1973. Ladd and Baron Von Raschke clobbered The Bruiser and The Crusher at Cobo Arena to win a WWA World Tag Team belt.

## Layton, Lord Athol (d. 1984)

We were shocked—*shocked*—to find while researching this book that Lord Layton was not a member of Great Britain's House of Lords. Heck, the Empire could have used Layton's lethal judo chop. Instead, Layton spent much of his career in Windsor, both as a host of Channel 9's *Big Time Wrestling* for some 15 years, and as an actor in the ring for many more. His regal bearing and English accent (Australian, awk-chew-ly) provided a skein of class to a sport in which participants regularly hit each other over the head with chairs.

Layton was born in Surrey, England, but moved to Sydney,

Australia, as a teenager. He quickly grew to his adult size of 6 feet 5 inches tall and 260 pounds, and was Australia's heavyweight boxing champ in his early 20s. After service in World War II with the Australian Imperial Forces, he ran a bar. When a gang of wrestlers stopped by Layton's town, Layton revived his interest in wrestling as a career.

He broke into the sport in Toronto in 1950—ironically, as a bad guy. His early career involved fighting Whipper Billy Watson, every Toronto lad's favorite. Layton's feud with Watson, unfortunately, spilled outside the ring. Layton's son, who was being taunted regularly by schoolyard colleagues who belonged to the Whipper Watson Safety Club, asked his dad to reconsider the Watson feud. "He asked me if it might be possible for me to join forces with Watson and become a tag team. Things would be more comfortable for him at school," Layton recalled in a 1981 interview with the *Toronto Sun.*

As a wrestler, Layton became an honest-to-goodness champ. He held several titles, including The Canadian Open Tag Team Title, which he held with Hans Hermann for a while in 1952, until Whipper Billy Watson and Pat Flanagan beat the duo. Layton later regained the title for three months in 1955—this time with his old foe, Whipper Billy Watson, as his tag team partner.

Detroiters remember Layton wrestling at Olympia Stadium or "air conditioned Cobo Arena," but even more remember his work on Channel 9's *Big Time Wrestling.* Wrestling was a regional form of entertainment at the time, and Layton had all of the heroes and villains of the Midwestern ring: Dick the Bruiser, The Sheik, Killer Kowalski, Professor Hiro, Fritz Von Erich and others. Even during the worst of the interviews, when his interviewees were spitting and cursing in his face, Layton never lost his cool.

But more than once, Layton abandoned his role as announcer and used his wrestling skills to correct what he judged to be unnecessary mayhem in the ring. A big Detroit television moment: Wrestler Johnny Valentine was torturing a foe with a figure-four leg lock, which the referee couldn't break up. Layton leapt into the ring and hit Valentine over the head with a microphone. This angered Valentine, who knocked Layton down and applied the figure-four move to the now-prone and groaning announcer. The stunt broke Layton's leg, providing interesting tape for the next week's edition of *Big Time Wrestling*.

Layton's own career in Detroit was memorable. A look at a Web site belonging to *Slam!,* a Canadian wrestling magazine, shows what people remembered most. "One great moment occurred when The Sheik's manager, the Weasel, provoked the Lord too far. Lord Layton dropped his microphone, ran into the ring and gave The Sheik a number of drop kicks, all with his suit and jacket on. Then, he ended it with a famous karate chop to The Weasel," wrote one correspondent.

That's entertainment.

## Sheik, The (d: 2003)

He threw fire. Sometimes, he hid jagged objects in his wrestling trunks and hacked at opponents. Sometimes, he hid razor blades in his boots. As wrestling scholar Steve Slagle noted: "Perhaps no other wrestler is more responsible for influencing the current generation of 'hardcore' wrestling than the one and only Arabian madman known as The Sheik."

The Sheik (real name: Edward Farhat) enraged Detroit wrestling fans during the 1950s and 1960s with his ruthless approach to the sport. The mere appearance of The Sheik would make fans crazy, inciting a tidal wave of heckling and jeering. The Sheik paid no heed. He'd mutter something. It sounded Arabic, but was actually gibberish mixed with a few Lebanese words. Once, when The Sheik had singed Bobo Brazil with a ball of flames, a man looked in amazement at his wife and said: "Honey, The Sheik done burned Boo-boo."

The Sheik with his manager Abdullah "The Weasel" Farouk.

76

Another memory comes from Brian Hyndman, of Toronto, on the Wrestling Canadian Hall of Fame Web site: "The Sheik … eating a page of (the interviewer's) interview notes, while his manager, Eddie 'The Brain' Creatchman, encouraged him to eat (the interviewer's) tie."

Farhat, a Lansing native, was the son of Lebanese immigrants. He used his background to fashion his bad guy wrestling persona: a rich guy from the Syrian upper class. Adding to the mayhem was Abdullah "the Weasel" Farouk (real name: Ernie Roth), who carried The Sheik's prayer rug. Roth was, in fact, Jewish.

Behind the persona was a savvy businessman. *Windsor Star* columnist Marty Gervais pointed out in an appreciation of The Sheik that the wrestler had lived in a $438,000 four-story home near Lansing, nestled on 37 acres.

The *New York Times* paid the Sheik the ultimate tribute by printing a meticulously detailed, two-column obituary at the time of his death. The country's newspaper of record, in its assessment of The Sheik's life, said that he "more or less single-handedly escalated the violence and commercial appeal of professional wrestling in the early years of television."

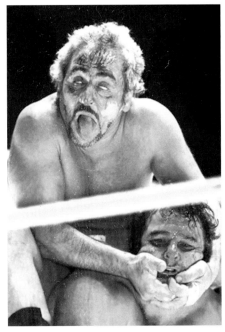

The Sheik: A man who loved his work.

## Valentine, Johnny (d: 2001)

Valentine (real name: John Theodore Wisniski) was wrestling's model bad guy. His many moves included the figure-four leg lock, a complicated maneuver which left Valentine's opponents limping from the ring; and the "brain buster," which wasn't complicated at all. The 6-feet 4-inch Valentine would crash his elbow atop the enemy's noggin.

The Seattle native broke into wrestling as a teenager. Detroit wrestling fans may remember him as Lord Layton's special nemesis, especially after Valentine beat Layton unconscious on camera one Saturday afternoon. A 1975 plane crash left him on crutches and unable to wrestle. According to several accounts,

Johnny Valentine preferred the figure-four leglock.

## The Tao of Wild Bull Curry

Announcer/wrestler Lord Layton and wrestler Wild Bull Curry mixed it up in this 1970 exchange.

**Layton**: Now, I want to get a bout with Ernie Ladd. I want to get a return bout with him. I don't ask a return bout with anybody, too often. But with Ladd, I do. Because I feel that somebody has got to stop...

**Curry**: Heeeeyyyyy. Wait a minute. Wait a minute.

**Layton**: And you're no better than him?

**Curry**: Aaaaaaayyy. Ha ha ha. Wait a minute.

**Layton**: Tell me what you were using in there.

**Curry**: None of your damned business. None of your business. Wait a minute.

**Layton**: It's business with me that you're going to hurt somebody...

**Curry**: I'm not going to hurt Bobo Brazil. I'm going to annihilate him. I'm going to ruin him, because I'm going to tell you something: Bobo Brazil you are what they call the champion that held the title the least, because I'm going to beat you on July 7...Bobo, I'm going to knock you're head off.

**Layton**: Well, you'd better get something heavier to hit him with than what he's using there. Fans, I think at this stage we're ready to go back for more wrestling.

medical bills left Valentine broke by the time of his death. That left Valentine's fans bitter, since they believed wrestling's multi-millionaire promoters should have taken care of Valentine. One wrestling writer, John F. Molinaro, quoted Bret Hart in describing Valentine's treatment: "We're like circus animals. And once we can't jump through hoops or do the same tricks we once could, promoters take us out back behind the circus tents and put a slug into us."

Valentine's son, Greg "The Hammer" Valentine, carries on.

## Von Erich, Fritz (d: 1997)

Fritz Von Erich (real name: Jack Adkisson) was a villain with a special talent for annoying fans—which is what wrestling fans enjoy most. Von Erich played the role of a Nazi in the ring—a palooka (6 feet 4 inches tall and 250 pounds) with the physical power of a Mack Truck and the finesse of a wrecking ball. His most feared hold was "the claw," in which Von Erich attached his claw to the opponent's midsection.

Von Erich started out playing football, first at Southern Methodist University and later with the American Football League's Dallas Texans. He was one of wrestling's biggest stars from the 1950s until his retirement in 1980.

Out of the ring, Von Erich led one of the most tragic lives imaginable. He buried five sons during his life. One died in Japan from an intestinal ailment, another overdosed on pills, two died from self-inflicted gunshot wounds, and another—a 7-year-old—accidentally electrocuted himself at the family farm.

Fritz Von Erich, conferring with an opponent, had a talent for annoying fans.

# Music

*Music has been an integral part of Detroit television from the very beginnings of the medium to the present day. And every kind of music was represented—from R&B to polka.*

## Club 1270

This was one of Detroit's '60s-era teen dance shows. Airing between 1963 and 1965, *Club 1270* was hosted variously by WXYZ-AM disc jockeys Lee Alan, Joel Sebastian (d: 1986) and Dave Prince—either alone or in some combination. It went live from Channel 7's Broadcast House every Saturday afternoon following ABC-TV's *American Bandstand*. Most significantly, Alan, Sebastian and Prince brought on virtually every important Motown act, plus the Rolling Stones and many national rock acts that came through town during the period. The Coasters and Dion helped with the debut show.

*Club 1270* was so successful that Channel 7 general manager John Pival created *The Swingin' Kind*, a series of three programs emceed by Alan in 1965. One show came from Detroit's Edgewater Amusement Park, another from Metropolitan Beach and a third from downtown Detroit's Michigan Consolidated Gas

*Club 1270's* Lee Alan (at left) with the Pixies Three and Joel Sebastian (right).

"Stosh" Wisniach, Detroit's polkameister.

Building. Performers included Stevie Wonder and Marvin Gaye. Pival and Alan had hopes of syndicating the program nationally. But Pival's festering problems with the ABC brass had become so acute that he was eventually sent packing. And when Pival went, so did the show's prospects.

## Club Polka

The beauty of local Detroit television during the early days was its tantalizing variety. The proof: Detroit had its own polka show on the air during the late 1940s and early 1950s. Hosted by Warren Michael Kelly, "Club Polka" featured accordionist Stan "Stosh" Wisniach and five colleagues.

Like many other Channel 7 shows, the effort was pioneered by John Pival, who discovered Wisniach while trolling for talent. Pival, along with Channel 7 band director Phil Brestoff and Dee "Auntie Dee" Parker, found Wisniach at the Tip Top Club, which has since been demolished.

As usual, Pival picked well. Wisniach had been playing professionally since the age of 10, developing his musical talents at the insistence of his father, a Ford Motor Co. assembly line worker who had better ideas for his son. Wisniach even became a fulltime employee of the station for a time in the early 1950s. He's still alive and, although confined to a wheelchair, still played in 2004.

Bud Davies once introduced Elvis to fans at the Fox Theatre.

## Davies, Bud

Davies was mostly a radio man, but he was also known for his work as host of CKLW-TV's *Top 10 Dance Party* in the mid-1950s. Davies was something of an institution at CKLW-AM. A Windsor native, he began his career at the station in the mailroom before World War II. After becoming a star in the 1950s, he exhibited a relentlessly pleasant persona, hosting shows such as *Your Boy Bud* and *Good Neighbor Club*. A bit of rock 'n' roll trivia: Davies introduced Elvis Presley at the Fox Theatre in the mid-1950s. Davies was let go from the station in 1966, even though he had nearly 30 years of seniority.

## McKenzie, Ed (d: 2001)

McKenzie, one of Detroit's top deejays during the 1950s and 1960s, also hosted local TV's first teen variety program—*The Ed McKenzie Saturday Party*. Deeper into his career, he helmed *After Hours*, a late-night talk show (it ran at about 1 a.m., after *Premiere Theatre*), in which he ruminated on everything from poetry and politics to philosophy. No topic was too obscure for McKenzie's encyclopedic intellect. He once discussed mushroom collecting in Moscow on the program.

McKenzie, popularly known as "Jack the Bellboy," was Detroit's first rock 'n' roll disc jockey. Heard on WJBK-AM from 1946 until 1952, and then on WXYZ-AM until 1959, he introduced a generation of white radio listeners to black music. The fame translated into the early medium of television, where he hosted *Saturday Dance Party* on Channel 7 between 1954 and 1958. Louis Armstrong and Chuck Berry were among McKenzie's guests.

Eventually, McKenzie grew weary of the radio business, and quit a $60,000-a-year job because he didn't like meddling in his program—complaining of "bad music, its incessant commercials in bad taste, its subservience to ratings and its pressures of payola."

## Parker, Dee (d: 2000)

*The Auntie Dee Show* was the prime exhibition spot for early 1950s Detroit youngsters who sang, danced, or otherwise had talent worthy of display. Parker started her professional life as a big-band singer who first came to the attention of Detroiters at downtown's Brass Rail nightclub. She and Channel 7 music chief Phil Brestoff later married.

Airing 4:30 p.m. weekdays, *The Auntie Dee Show* featured youngsters who would sing, dance or play musical instruments.

Rock 'n' roll deejay Ed McKenzie (left) with musician George Young.

Dee Parker huddles with a young star.

Writer Howard Buten described her as "a bouncy blonde sweetheart determined to hunt out every ounce of burgeoning talent this side of Cobo Hall." Uncle Jimmie Stevenson accompanied the acts on a piano. Singer Ursula Walker and traffic reporter Jo-Jo Shutty-MacGregor both appeared on the program.

Former *Detroit News* editorial writer George Cantor remembered appearing on the program Good Friday, 1952. His experience wasn't unusual. Cantor, a 10-year-old fifth grader at Detroit's Roosevelt Elementary School, took the Dexter Avenue bus with his three buddies to Channel 7's studio in the Maccabees Building. "This wasn't a contest—she wouldn't stand for that," Cantor recalls. The quartet sang "The Syncopated Clock." Also on the show that day was a young African-American youngster who sang "The Lord's Prayer." Cantor remembers this as unusual because African-American faces were not regularly seen on television.

The show lasted until 1956. Parker and Brestoff moved to Los Angeles. She later moved to the San Francisco area, where she lived until her death in 2000. "All the way until the end, when music was played, she would be in the front singing and waving her hands in the breeze," her son, Nelson Brestoff, told the *Detroit Free Press.* "Just as a fish swims in water, my mother reacted to music the same way. That's how she thrived."

## Scene, The

As writer Jim McFarlin so aptly wrote in *The Michigan Front Page,* this Channel 62 dance show was "the most popular Detroit TV series no one would admit to watching." Compared to the dancers on *The Scene*, dancers on Channel 9's old *Swingin' Time* looked positively wooden, if not dead. "I think the significance of *The Scene* was that it represented pure, 100 percent uncut black culture for a certain period of time in Detroit," host Nat Morris told McFarlin. "When I look

*The Scene* became the epicenter of Detroit hipdom during the '70s and '80s.

back and think about it now, we were exposing the culture of Detroit of the day."

Morris grew up in North Carolina and trained for the broadcast business in New York City. He came to Flint in 1972, and was hired later that year by program director George White at WGPR-TV. WGPR-FM deejay Ray Henderson recommended Morris, with Henderson serving as co-host of *The Scene*.

Nobody else in local television these days would have the guts to put on a show like *The Scene*. Young Detroiters, virtually all African-American, would dance at Channel 62's studios on East Jefferson Avenue, a converted auto dealership on Detroit's east side. The clothing was always original, the dancing always at least 15 minutes ahead of its time. The important thing was that the youngsters who appeared on the show were themselves. "We told the guests to dress like they were going out on Saturday night," Morris recalls. Other than that, there were no instructions. The guests danced and acted as themselves. And, of course, the show's "bootycam"—an extreme version of the "Honey Shots" that the late Roone Arledge popularized on ABC's *Monday Night Football*—was a topic of discussion.

This was required viewing for anybody who aspired to any sort of hipness during the 1970s and 1980s. And it provided a window into Detroit's African-American culture. The show went off the air in 1987, after 12 years. As of 2004, people were still talking about the show. "We're talking about doing a 30-year reunion in 2005," says Morris, who now runs a video production company, appropriately called The Scene. "People won't let it die."

Part of the Detroit iconography: "Sugar is sugar, and salt is salt. And if you didn't get off, it's not our fault."

## Seymour, Robin

As host of Channel 9's *Swingin' Time*, he was Detroit's most important teenage tastemeister. Bob Seger was introduced to the

*The Scene* host Nat Morris (right).

*Swingin' Time* host Robin Seymour.

Motor City television audience playing "East Side Story." Seymour also introduced Detroiters to Motown music. To this day, he says it was one of his greatest accomplishments.

Seymour, a graduate of Central High School, studied radio at Wayne State University before inaugurating his *Bobbin' with Robin* show on WKMH (later WKNR) in 1947, when Seymour was all of 20 years old. When rock 'n' roll became big, Seymour made the transition—although not without some difficulty. In 1956, Seymour predicted that Elvis Presley would be an unknown by 1957. The gaffe wasn't fatal, however. Some 9,000 teenagers once showed up to watch Seymour interview Sal Mineo at Edgewater Park.

By the early 1960s, teen dance shows with local hosts began popping up all over the country. Cleveland, for instance, had Lloyd Thaxton. Seymour, noting the popularity of Philadelphia's Dick Clark, started a Channel 9 dance show, *Teen Town*, in 1964. *Teen Town* later morphed into *Swingin' Summertime*, and then into *Swingin' Time*, which became "must see" TV for teens long before NBC popularized the phrase. Most rock groups of any consequence appeared on the program—with or without their instruments. The Lovin' Spoonful couldn't get their instruments across the border before one appearance, so they appeared with cardboard guitars and drums. When WKNR management forced Seymour to choose between his radio gig and his Channel 9 job, Seymour stuck with Channel 9. By 1968, a year when Jimi Hendrix and Cream were the working definition of hip, Seymour was a middle-aged man in a tie and Armani suit. He became an anomaly, even if he could shake it up on the dance floor with the kids. Tom Shannon replaced Seymour in 1968. Seymour grew a mustache and tried another local dance show, but it didn't work.

After broadcasting, Seymour moved to California and launched a career in marketing and sales.

## Surrell, Jack (d: 2003)

Surrell hosted *Sunday With Surrell*, a 1950s-era television show that featured African-American performers from the Detroit area. He was also heard on WXYZ radio, where he hosted one of the hippest programs in the 1950s. As former radio station manager Dick Kernen recalled to Dick Osgood in a book about WXYZ radio and television: "Jack Surrell, as I recall, was into a little more sophisticated music than the rest of the station. I don't think it was necessarily black music 'cause at the time Jack was on the air there was no black consciousness. Most people thought Surrell was white; most people were astounded to find he was black." His trademark: Surrell opened with "Penthouse Serenade," and closed with "Night Train."

Raised in Philadelphia, Surrell studied music at Temple University. According to a *Detroit Free Press* obituary, he came to Detroit in the 1930s. At times, he worked for Pearl Bailey, Ethel Waters and Bill (Bojangles) Robinson. Ed McKenzie discovered Surrell playing piano in an area nightclub. When Stroh Brewery made a push to sell beer in Detroit's growing African-American community, Surrell found a sponsor for his radio show. Surrell was probably more famous for his radio work, but belongs in the history books for breaking the color barrier in Detroit television.

*Sunday with Surrell* was certainly a groundbreaking effort for jazz on television. Detroit was known nationally as a major center for jazz during the early 1950s, and Surrell's show boosted that reputation and encouraged budding musicians. Guitarist Kenny Burrell was a member of Surrell's in-house band.

Although Surrell's television show lasted only a few years, his music career continued almost until his death in 2003. By day, he worked at a tank plant in Warren. At night, he played at Dearborn's Chicago Road House. In the years before his death, he released two CDs of his music.

Jack Surrell, famous for his radio work, also hosted a '50s-era TV show.

# News

*Local television news, at least in theory,*
*tells a community about itself. This is the group that did that job,*
*reflecting Detroit's image back to viewers.*

## American Black Journal

Channel 56's *American Black Journal* was born in the after-math of the 1967 Detroit riots, mostly as an effort to finally give Detroit's African-American citizens a place on television. The show's first title was *CPT(Colored People's Time)*, and featured Tony Brown at the helm. More than three decades later, the show still airs—although under the less tongue-in-cheek title.

The program evolved into a forum for African-American intel-lectuals to discuss their work. Some of the guests have included writers Alex Haley, Terri McMillan and James Baldwin, film-maker Robert Townsend, musician Branford Marsalis, Motown mogul Berry Gordy Jr., and talk show host Ken Hamblin.

*ABJ* also turned into a springboard for African-American broadcasters. Brown went on to become a nationally recognized writer and lecturer. During the 1980s, its host was Ed Gordon, who later went on to Black Entertainment Television, and then

NBC News. Darryl Wood replaced Gordon, and was the show's anchor into the 21st century.

## Bennett, Bob (d: 2004)

Bennett was a mainstay at Channel 4's news department for more than three decades, between 1968 and 2000. By the time he retired, he was the opposite of a lot of TV street reporters. Most were young, thin and inexperienced. Bennett was not young (he was 61 when he announced his retirement), not thin and had journalism chops going back to City Hall in the 1960s. It showed. "I think the reason he clicks on the air is that he's so real," said Ben Burns, director of Wayne State University's journalism program. "He reports straightforwardly and accurately. You don't get any unnecessary drama introduced by Bob." Colleague Dwayne X. Riley goes one step further: "He's a walking book of knowledge. The background resources of a television station are limited, to say the least. But whenever we needed to know something—who was elected to Detroit City Council and when, for instance—we depended on his knowledge."

A native of Indianapolis, Bennett joined WCHB-AM in 1962 as a newsman and gospel disc jockey. It was there that he worked with Martha Jean "The Queen" Steinberg. Channel 4 took a run at hiring Bennett in the mid-1960s, but his bosses at WCHB-AM upped his pay by $50 a week. He jumped to WXYZ-AM in 1965 and was pursued by Channel 7. However, Channel 4 also continued to woo Bennett and snared him in May 1968. At the time, he was the station's second African-American reporter. (The first was Jerry Blocker.)

Bennett quickly earned a reputation for hard work, spending five days a week at Channel 4 while doing news on WWJ-AM on Saturdays. In one of his biggest scoops, he broke the story of the 1969 arrest of John Norman Collins, a suspect in the sensational coed serial murders in the Ann Arbor area. Many print and broad-

Bob Bennett (left) on the case.

cast journalists regarded him as one of the most respected newsmen in Detroit. "I think he's one of the deans of local television news," said MSNBC's Mike Huckman.

That respect extends to City Hall. Bennett was a reporter when many in Detroit's power circle were coming up. One such case is former Detroit City Council President Gil Hill, who was a street cop when he got to know Bennett in the 1960s. "You know how cops are about reporters," commented Hill, "they don't like to say much. But nobody ever had any hesitation about talking to Bob Bennett. He was unfailingly fair and accurate, never violated a confidence and never took a cheap shot. I don't know of anybody who said they were screwed by Bob Bennett. And you can't say that about many reporters."

Despite the respect in which he is held, the final years of his career saw him in front of fire scenes or outside in blizzards.

For some reason, the assignment editors at Channel 4 couldn't think of a better way to utilize him—like assigning Jascha Heifetz to play "Louie Louie" on the violin. Detroit journalism might have been better if Bennett was allowed to exercise his full talent.

He had offers from Chicago, New York, Denver and Los Angeles, but stayed in Detroit. "Detroit is in my blood," Bennett said. "It's been a love/hate thing—mostly love."

## Biscoe, Doris

She was one of Detroit's first African-American female anchors, joining Channel 7 in 1973. Biscoe lasted on the air for 25 years, and became one of the town's most recognizable faces. Twenty-five years in Detroit broadcasting is an amazing feat, given the unstable nature of the television business. However, Biscoe was taken off the air within months of celebrating a quarter-century in television, in 1998.

Biscoe was educated at Washington, D.C.'s Howard University. She worked in Washington radio and modeled (she's

Channel 7's Doris Biscoe.

5 feet 11 inches) before pursuing a television career. A relative—former Wayne County Sheriff William Lucas—suggested to Channel 7 news director Phil Nye that he take a look at Biscoe's audition tape. "He told me, 'Look, I don't know if she's got it or not, but I'd appreciate it if you'd at least give her a look,'" Nye recalls. After signing on as a reporter on Channel 7's late news, Biscoe anchored the station's 6 p.m., noon and early morning newscasts. Joanne Purtan replaced Biscoe as co-anchor of Channel 7's 5:30–7 a.m. newscast. Biscoe now performs occasional public relations work.

## Blake, Asha

This former Channel 4 anchor co-anchored NBC News' *Later Today*, which was killed after only one year on the air. She had been anchoring Channel 4's weekend newscasts and working as a medical reporter between 1993 and 1996 when two networks—NBC and ABC—came calling. (She landed at ABC, but jumped to NBC News a few years later.) "Quite frankly, we probably wouldn't have left had the networks not come calling. … It was one of those opportunities you couldn't turn down. And Carmen (Harlan, the station's longtime female lead anchor) wasn't leaving. There wasn't a lot of upward mobility at the station. The people above—whom I like very much—weren't going anywhere. My three years in Detroit were the best in my life."

Blake started out in the news business in Little Rock, Arkansas, and Grand Junction, Colorado, before joining KARE-TV in Minneapolis. She injured herself while exercising and was laid up for three months. That experience drove her to medical reporting, which she excelled in after joining Channel 4 in 1993.

After leaving Channel 4, Blake worked as a co-anchor of ABC News' *World News Now* and *World News This Morning*. In the fall of 1999, she joined Jodi Applegate and Florence Henderson as part of the troika that hosted the short-lived *Later Today*. As of this writing, she hosts *Life Moments*, a syndicated program that airs locally on Channel 62.

## Blocker, Jerry (d: 2000)

Blocker, who joined Channel 4 in 1967, was Detroit's first African-American television reporter. A Detroit native and 1959 graduate of Northwestern High School, Blocker had always wanted to get into broadcasting—even as a child. But his mother warned him, he says, about trying to make it "in the white-folks field."

After graduation from Wayne State University in 1953, he found his mother was right. At one Detroit radio audition, Blocker recalled "they put scripts in front of me that included nothing but classical music terms. Unless you know a lot about classical music, it's like reading in a foreign language. So I didn't do well." Instead, he taught at an elementary school in Detroit's Cass Corridor and continued knocking on doors.

He finally landed a job in 1960 at WCHD-FM (now WCHB-FM). Blocker was finally brought in for an interview at Channel 4 a few weeks after the 1967 Detroit riots. Many thought Blocker's hiring had to do with the embarrassing fact that Detroit had no African-American TV reporters to cover the biggest racial story in the city's history. That, however, isn't true. Channel 4's executives, who had been reading U.S. Census reports and noticed the town's changing ethnic character, had been contemplating the move.

Recalled Blocker: "We didn't know how I was going to be accepted by blacks or whites. It was quite a gamble. … None of this came easy. The social and financial realities finally seeped their way up to the top management."

Once at Channel 4, Blocker earned respect from the management for his tenacity and hard work. He'd started out as the education reporter. After a short time, the station's general manager

Channel 4's Jerry Blocker was Detroit's first African-American anchorman.

decided that Blocker should anchor the news. Blocker protested that he did not yet have enough television experience to do the job properly. The station's general manager thought otherwise. In an effort to prepare for the anchor job, Blocker spent roughly two months "woodshedding" in Channel 4's wire room, reading copy and practicing his delivery. After leaving Channel 4, he worked as a news director at Channel 62, and then in the political advertising business.

## Bonds, Bill

He was the first on-air television news personality to realize the medium's dramatic possibilities. Before Bonds, Dick Westerkamp, Carl Cederberg and Jac Le Goff were the norm: They were solid, credible, informed and unexcitable, unemotional. These are all fine qualities for a newsman. But the television medium's potential for dramatic communication was untapped.

Bonds grew up on 12th Street near Burlingame. Congenitally argumentative and intellectually curious, these qualities were not much appreciated in his youth. He was kicked out of one Catholic school after another and earned mediocre grades. He joined the U.S. Army, graduated from the University of Detroit and worked at a string of radio stations, usually just at the edge of breaking through. WJR-AM executives took a look at him but passed. Bonds auditioned for Channel 4 news director Jim Clark, who opined that Bonds didn't quite have the stuff to make it in television. Sonny Eliot arranged for an interview with other TV executives, but Bonds didn't show.

What broke him out of the radio business and into television was part serendipity. Bonds had been working as a City Hall reporter for WKNR-AM, then considered one of the better broadcast news operations in Detroit. Bonds was tenacious. Covering a tornado in Anchor Bay and unable to feed his story to the station, Bonds climbed a telephone pole, used alligator clips to hook to

color

All the news, sports and weather in a concise 15 minute package.

**BILL BONDS NEWS**

⑦ WXYZ-TV 6:30 & 11 PM MON–FRI

Channel 7's Bill Bonds in his glum anchorman mode.

the station, and reported his stories. His first newscast of the day was 4:45 a.m. He'd do the morning news, then head out to cover Detroit City Council and City Hall. Mayor Jerome P. Cavanagh liked Bonds and even offered him a job as a speechwriter. ("I didn't take it, "Bonds later recalled, "because my ego would have gotten in the way. I thought I should be the guy making policy.") Channel 7 general manager John Pival had gotten orders from ABC's New York brass to develop a serious news department. Pival was on the plane back from New York with the orders. Cavanagh was on the flight with Pival, and suggested he take a look at Bonds. Bonds was hired, and found a home.

After a few years as a street reporter, Bonds was named anchorman. The 1967 Detroit riots changed the lives of many Detroiters, but it changed Bonds' more than most. He shone with his heartfelt commentary and aggressive coverage. The ratings began going up. ABC brass had found their star. With the exception of stays in Los Angeles during the late 1960s/early 1970s and New York City for less than a year in the mid-1970s, Bonds became Channel 7's icon—and most famous employee. Everything fell into place: ABC's traditionally weak prime-time lineup became strong as Channel 7's staff of on-air reporters and front-office executives shaped the station's newscast into one of the hardest-hitting journalistic products in town. At the zenith of his power during the early 1980s, literally half of the televisions switched on at 11 p.m. would be switched to Bonds. By the early 1990s, the station wanted him badly enough that they signed him to a $1 million-per-year contract that should have taken him to a graceful retirement.

Unfortunately, his retirement was anything but graceful. Bonds' drinking, which had always been a problem, mushroomed into a crisis. He challenged Mayor Coleman Young to a fistfight on the air. (What was not publicized was Bonds' visit to Young's office later, where Bonds personally apologized to the mayor.) There

At the peak of Bonds' career, Channel 7 captured half of the 11 p.m. news audience.

**On October 16, 1991, Bill Bonds engaged in a verbal mud-wrestling match with U.S. Senator Orrin Hatch (R-Utah). This is the transcript of the interview, which ended with Hatch walking out.**

**Bonds**: I have to say to you, sir, just as an American from the Midwest, that frankly, you and your colleagues on the Senate Judiciary Committee—with some of your cheap shots at one another—that was kind of an embarrassing spectacle. Do you regret that that went on?

**Hatch**: Well, I didn't see any real cheap shots. You know it was a tense, difficult process, as it should be. And it was made even worse because of one dishonest senator who leaked raw FBI data that then became public.

**Bonds**: Senator, you guys leak all the time.

**Hatch**: No, that's not true.

**Bonds**: Who are you trying to kid? You guys leak stuff all the time.

**Hatch**: Let me just say something: That's not true.

**Bonds**: Yes it is.

**Hatch**: No, not FBI reports from the Judiciary Committee. Look, I've been there 15 years. I know what's going on.

**Bonds**: There are guys who say you've been there too long.

**Hatch**: That could be. In 15 years, I have not seen leaks of FBI reports because they contain raw data. They contain raw information of people who are crazy, people who hate each other, people who have axes to grind, and that's why they don't do that, and we've always honored that. This time they did not. And the bad thing

was that everybody knew about this report before the vote. Senator Biden had explained it to every Democrat. Everybody on the committee, each person could have put it over for a week.

**Bonds**: OK, your conduct was great. You guys all look terrific. Two hundred fifty million Americans are really proud of Senator Orrin Hatch and all the rest of you guys.

**Hatch**: I'm not, I'm not...

**Bonds**: You did a marvelous job, we're all proud of you. You never made the country look better. Let me ask you something: What are you going to do if you find out six months from now that Clarence Thomas, who you've just about made into a saint, is a porno freak?

**Hatch**: Don't worry, we won't. But I'll tell you: If you're going to interview us in the future, you ought to be at least courteous. I think you're about as discourteous a person as I've ever, ever interviewed with. I don't like you, and I don't like what you are doing. If you don't like what we're saying, if you don't like what we're doing, then say so. But don't act that way with me.

**Bonds**: Well, I didn't vote for you, Senator.

**Hatch**: Well, I appreciate that. But don't act like that with me. Look, I go through enough crap back here, I don't have to go through it with you. Let me tell you something.

**Bonds**: No, let me tell you something...

**Hatch**: No, you tell yourself something. I'm tired of talking to you.

**Bonds**: OK, fine. I'm tired of talking to you. See you later.

was a well-publicized stay in rehab, and a couple of unpublicized ones. The business had become increasingly money oriented. Although Bonds had gotten rich from television, he became increasingly alienated from what the business had become.

His home, the Channel 7 newsroom, had become somebody's ATM machine. He'd rage when he'd walk into another TV station and see writers doing their work with computers, while Channel 7's writers still wrote on typewriters. In the end, he sank beneath successive tidal waves of fatigue, frustration, fury and drink. A drunken driving arrest one Sunday morning ended his Channel 7 career, seemingly permanently.

There were other outings after that: a stint as an interviewer and anchorman at Channel 2; as a commentator again at Channel 7. It ended with Bonds leaving to do commercials for Gardner-White Furniture, a quiet end to a noisy career.

## Caputo, Vic

Caputo worked as an anchorman and morning news host at Channel 2 for a dozen years between 1968 and 1980. During several of those years, he was paired with Woody Willis on both the station's early and late news. Oftentimes, he worked the lighter side of the news. He once wore Sydney Greenstreet's old suit for a showing of *Casablanca*, and was made up as an ape by the makeup man from *Planet of the Apes*.

Caputo abandoned it all—the TV career, Greenstreet's suit and the ape makeup—to run for U.S. Congress on metro Detroit's east side in 1980. After being beaten by Democrat Dennis Hertel, Caputo went to work in Tucson as a TV newsman.

## Carrier, Betty

She was Detroit's first lead female anchor, although the experiment only lasted about seven months. A Detroit native and a graduate of Wayne State University, Carrier started out at Pontiac's WPON-AM and as a press relations person at the United Foundation until she was hired at Channel 4 in late 1969.

In 1973, Channel 4's managers decided to take a chance with Carrier at the anchor desk. The women's liberation movement

Channel 2's Vic Caputo.

was in full force, and some thought putting a woman in a key role at 6 p.m. and 11 p.m. would help the station's ratings. She worked with the team of Dean Miller, Sonny Eliot and Jim Forney.

It didn't work. She got the job in April, but moved back to the lower-profile newscasts by late November. *Detroit Free Press* TV writer Bettelou Peterson told readers: "…the ladies have to remember that equal chance means equal hazard, too … There is too much money and prestige involved in the acceptance of the local newscasts to play it altogether noble." In 1974, she left the station to have a son.

## Cederberg, Carl

A Detroit television pioneer, he was on the ground floor of the development of Channel 2's news department. When he joined Channel 2 in 1960, he wasn't *a* newscaster. He was *the* news-caster—as in nobody but Cederberg spoke on camera. By the time he left the station in 1974, the station had one of the best TV news operations in town—and more than one person to read the news.

A native of Bay City, Cederberg got his start in broadcasting as a high schooler working part-time at a Bay City/Saginaw radio station. He recalls reading war news over the public address system to his fellow students after Pearl Harbor. It wasn't much of a stretch when he signed on during World War II with the Armed Forces Radio Services, where he broadcast the news from Milne Bay, New Guinea and the Pacific.

After the war, he landed a job at WWJ-AM. "Actually, I stopped by the station to see the studios, because I'd heard they were state-of-the-art," he later recalled. "But the receptionist told me they didn't give tours, and the only way for me to see the equipment was to come in and audition." He was hired.

In addition to anchoring key radio newscasts, Cederberg worked on Channel 4's early television news endeavors. He

Channel 2's Carl Cederberg.

signed on at Channel 2 in 1960 to replace Jac Le Goff, who had been canned in late 1959 for an editorial on payola scandals in the rock radio business. When Cederberg signed on at Channel 2, the news department consisted of a part-time news director and a photographer. That was it. Putting on a newscast consisted of retrieving film from Metro Airport that CBS News had shot, and scurrying about for whatever news the meager staff could muster.

During his 14 years at Channel 2, Cederberg served as an anchorman, news director, managing editor and news editor. He later went to work at the NBC affiliate in Lansing/Jackson/Battle Creek, where he worked with Robbie Timmons. During the 1990s, he worked as a newscaster at Ann Arbor's WAAM-AM.

## Cline, Ken (d: 1979)

You saw his face, but fans of local TV were more familiar with his voice. Channel 2's Ken Cline was the station's booth announcer during the 1950s and 1960s—the guy who did the station breaks, or said, "It's 11 o'clock. Do you know where your children are?" The job has been rendered largely obsolete by computer technology. At the time, however, the booth announcer was a key position.

A native of Oklahoma, Cline joined Storer Broadcasting's WJBK-AM as news director in 1948, the same year television hit Detroit. Cline switched to Storer's new TV station, Channel 2, shortly thereafter. Cline had two jobs throughout the 1950s and 1960s: He would handle Saturday evening chores while Jac Le Goff anchored weekdays. When newsman Carl Cederberg joined the station in 1960, Cederberg did the news Sundays through Fridays while Cline continued with the Saturday shift. Cline switched full-time to booth announcing in 1965, a job he held until the fall of 1978. He died of cancer in 1979.

## Crim, Mort

The Boy Scout pledge suggests that a good Scout leaves things better than when they got there. That being the case, Mort Crim is the ultimate Boy Scout. When he arrived at Channel 4, the station's 11 p.m. newscast was in third place, and not doing much better during the late afternoon and evening hours. When he left almost 20 years later, the station was in first place at 11 p.m.—and doing quite nicely at other times. Crim, a leader at the station both on the air and off, deserves a sizable amount of the credit.

Crim had already enjoyed considerable success as a newscaster before his hiring in 1978 as Post-Newsweek's new top gun in Detroit. He had worked at the ABC Radio network, where Peter Jennings and Ted Koppel were colleagues. He had successfully anchored in Philadelphia, a city bigger than Detroit. He had subbed for ABC's Paul Harvey. Crim had been in Chicago for a year when Channel 4 news director Jim Snyder persuaded him to come to Detroit. Even after he got here, ABC News seriously thought of hiring Crim as one of its top anchors. According to Marc Gunther's *The House That Roone Built*, ABC News president Roone Arledge seriously considered adding Crim to the Peter Jennings/Frank Reynolds team. Max Robinson was chosen instead. Later, Arledge offered Crim the weekend anchor job at *World News Tonight*, but suggested that Crim would also cover Capitol Hill during the week. Realizing the damage the schedule would do to his family life, Crim turned the job down.

The heavy-duty background somehow worked against Crim, rather than for him. He was tacitly accused of being a "carpetbagger." At some point, Detroiters realized Crim was serious about this town, and really took to him.

He retired to run a production company, write books and do radio commentary.

Carmen Harlan and Mort Crim became one of the most successful teams in Detroit television news history.

*President Lyndon B. Johnson created the Kerner Commission in 1967 to study the outbreak of rioting in this country's African-American neighborhoods five days after rioting and looting began in Detroit. The commission looked at local television news coverage in Detroit and elsewhere. Here's what the commission had to say about Detroit:*

"About one-third of all riot-related sequences for network and local appeared on the first day following the outbreak of rioting, regardless of the course of development of the riot itself. After the first day there was, except in Detroit, a very sharp decline in the amount of television time devoted to the disturbance. In Detroit, where the riot started slowly and did not flare out of control until July 24, 48 hours after it started, the number of riot-related sequences shown increased until July 26, and then showed the same sharp drop-off as noted after the first day of rioting in other cities. (Footnote: Detroit news outlets substantially refrained from publicizing the riot during the early part of Sunday, the first day of rioting.) These findings tend to controvert the impression that the riot intensifies television coverage, thus in turn intensifying the riot. The content analysis indicates that whether or not the riot was getting worse, television coverage of the riot decreased sharply after the first day."

**This is what Channel 4 viewers heard at 1 a.m. the morning of July 27, 1967.**

"The streets of Detroit could well be called War Zone D this morning. Tanks rumble along the city's main streets. Helicopters whirl overhead, some of them coming under fire. This darkness is punctuated by the flashes of rifle barrels as snipers and some of the 12,000 troops in Detroit exchange gunfire. These are the sights and sounds of the worst riot in the nation's history, about to enter its fifth day.

"The frightening toll has been mounting almost by the hour, even though military leaders and reporters both agree things are relatively calm compared with the trouble of the last few nights. At last count, 38 persons had been killed. The latest, a white looter shot while fleeing an east side auto parts store."

*Report of the National Advisory Commission on Civil Disorders.* New York: Bantam Books, 1968.

## Detroit Week In Review

This was Channel 56's weekly public affairs show, 1981-1989. Anchored by *Detroit Free Press* managing editor Neal Shine, the one-hour Friday night program featured journalists talking about stories they covered during the week. A frequent guest was WJR-AM's Bill Black, whose encyclopedic intellect often made him the star of the broadcast. Usually, Shine's guests included a *Free*

*Detroit Free Press* managing editor, Neal Shine, anchored *Detroit Week in Review.*

*Press* reporter (*Detroit News* management boycotted the show at first, but later rescinded the boycott), a radio reporter and a Detroit correspondent from one of the out-of-town publications, such as the *New York Times*. Journalists received $35 for their appearances. Shine received $50.

Although the show's guests were often not polished, on-the-air broadcasters, the raw quality made it a cult hit among news junkies who wondered what the faces behind the bylines looked like. It was cancelled in 1989, but Shine continued with *Neal Shine's Detroit* for another year.

## Dohrs, Dr. Fred E.

Long before talk radio made conservatism a mainstream political force, Dr. Fred E. Dohrs launched his conservative tirades on Detroit's airwaves. During Watergate and Vietnam, he was hired at Channel 4 by the Evening News Association to counterbalance what the ENA perceived was a liberal bias from NBC News. The segment was called *Newswatch*, and it anticipated the point of view later popularized by radio's Rush Limbaugh. Dohrs caught the tenor of the era. Vice President Spiro Agnew excoriated the TV networks and East Coast newspapers as elitist and maybe even secretly subversive. (Remember the phrase "nattering nabobs of negativity"?)

Dohrs' day job was as a geography professor at Wayne State University. His specialty was politics, culture and geography. One of his books, *World Regional Geography: A Problem Approach*, can still be found in WSU's library.

What people didn't know—but people on the WSU campus suspected—was that Dohrs worked with the Central Intelligence Agency. While Dohrs vacationed one summer, an invitation showed up in his Channel 4 mailbox to a black-tie dinner at the White House with President Richard Nixon. News Director Jim Clark, worried that Dohrs would miss the event, took the trouble to track down Dohrs. Clark found him at Central Intelligence Agency headquarters in Langley, Virginia.

## Eubanks, Dayna

She co-anchored Channel 7's evening newscasts with Bill Bonds between 1985 and 1988. However, tension with Bonds caused problems on the set—notably when she corrected Bonds on the air one night. While she may have been journalistically correct, it turned out to be career suicide. Her contract at Channel 7 was not renewed and she ended up at Channel 2, where she hosted one of the lowest-rated talk shows on television.

Eubanks, a graduate of the University of Kansas, worked in Topeka and Phoenix before arriving in Detroit for an 11-year stay. During that time, she worked as a reporter on Channel 7's *Good Afternoon, Detroit* program. Station management put her in the fast lane, giving her Diana Lewis' slot on the 11 p.m. newscast. The job lasted three years.

Eubanks anchors the news at Cincinnati's WKRC-TV.

## Feldman, Murray

Feldman signed on with Channel 2 in 1976, and has since weathered a succession of owners, general managers, news directors and journalistic philosophies. Perhaps Feldman lasts because of one unchanging verity: Viewers like their news delivered straight, by someone who knows what they're talking about. Feldman specializes in business and financial news, which he delivers in an earnest, straightforward style. As of this writing, he also co-anchors the station's 5:30 p.m. newscasts, and is heard regularly on WWJ-AM.

A native of Philadelphia and a graduate of Boston's Emerson College, Feldman worked in Providence, Rhode Island, and Syracuse, New York, before news director Dick Graf brought him to Detroit.

## Femmel, Dick

Femmel was a vital figure in the early days of Channel 7 news. A graduate of Northwestern University's Medill School of Journalism, he was initially hired as a news writer at WXYZ radio. He eventually became Channel 7's news director, a job that came with a significant roadblock. Channel 7 general manager John Pival wasn't interested in news, which tied Femmel's hands. "We never had a budget to do anything," Femmel told writer Dick Osgood. "It was always clinging to news by your fingernails."

Pival presented other problems, as well. Femmel's agenda was journalism, while Pival's was show business. He later wrote editorials for Pival, leaving the station in 1965 to work with George Pierrot. In one of the strange twists of the television business, Pival became the architect of Channel 7's news image, driving his troops to heights no one else foresaw. Femmel finished his professional career as a vice president at Blue Cross Blue Shield and a journalism teacher at Wayne State University.

## Fisher, Rich

He's anchored the news on three Detroit TV stations in a career that spanned the 1980s, the 1990s and the 2000s. If Bill Bonds and Mort Crim were the anchor "gods" of their era, Fisher was an anchor "demi-god"—quite near, but not quite at the top. A native of Detroit and the son of a Detroit policeman, he learned broadcast journalism in Alpena and Flint before joining Channel 7, where he became something of an understudy to Bill Bonds at the anchor desk. Fisher subbed for Bonds when Bonds landed in a rehab facility in the late 1980s. It's a credit to Fisher and the Channel 7 news operation that the ratings didn't suffer when Bonds was away. Fisher relocated to Channel 2 (1990-1997), and later to Channel 50 (2000-2002), where he replaced David Scott.

Unfortunately, Fisher learned the down side of being on TV: A *Detroit News* gossip columnist made great hay out of Fisher's failing marriage and active dating habits in the mid-1980s. Later, his $2,000 contribution to then-U.S. Senator Spencer Abraham's political campaign attracted attention. (Journalists are supposed to be unbiased, and usually don't contribute to campaigns.)

As of this writing, Fisher is out of TV news.

## Frazier, Ben

Frazier was one of the most intriguing "coulda-beens" in the history of Detroit television.

He co-anchored Channel 4's 6 p.m. and 11 p.m. newscasts in 1980-81 with Mort Crim. Ratings were up. Frazier's confident style and perfectly modulated baritone were certainly appealing. Only in his early 30s, Frazier could have owned the town if he'd hung in for awhile.

What happened was that Frazier made what he later told *Detroit Free Press* reporter Ellen Creager were "some pretty bad choices." Hoping for a pay raise and acting on advice from his agent, Frazier phoned in sick with "neck problems" during the fall of 1981. The station's management insisted that Frazier's absence was a clumsy attempt at cadging money. Wrote *Detroit News* television writer Ben Brown: "It (the brouhaha) is not about people being dumped on. It's not about racism. It's not even about television. The issue is money. Frazier wants more of it; Channel 4 doesn't want to pay it."

Whatever the case, Channel 4 news director Jim Snyder put Carmen Harlan in Frazier's chair, where she has been ever since. That attracted picketers to Channel 4, insisting Frazier's fate was a "racially motivated demotion and unconscionable treatment." He later hosted Channel 56's *Detroit Black Journal* before leaving for Florida in 1985.

What happened later was not pretty. Frazier's wife, Josephine, told the *Free Press'* Creager that cocaine was to blame for later problems.

## Free 4 All

This Channel 4 public affairs show introduced anchorman Mort Crim to the Detroit audience. "Mort had gotten here but nobody knew who he was, other than that he had a booming voice. We needed to show him walking around talking to an audience," recalls Harvey Ovshinsky, one of the show's creators. To that end, Channel 4 producers created a sort of Noah's Ark of Detroit opinion: There was one of everything. Five panelists debated issues in front of a live audience while Crim guided the show. Ovshinsky once described the show to *Detroit Free Press* TV critic Mike Duffy as a "*What's My Line* panel *Meets the Press* in front of a *Donahue* audience." Duffy, in a 1981 review, called the show "informative and entertaining."

The five cast members had included Mike Sessa, who was active in the state's tax cut movement; Larry Simmons, an Urban League staffer; Diane Trombley, a registered nurse who also worked in the pro-life movement; Joan Israel, who was active in the National Organization for Women; and Janice Burnett, a former mental health worker. Unlike shows of this type of later years, the guests did more than yell at each other—although there was some of that. Crim's wit and personality became apparent to the Detroit viewing audience.

Dennis Archer, who later became Detroit's mayor, auditioned for a post on the show but didn't get it. "Nice guy, but not compelling enough," recalls Ovshinsky. Mike Sessa was later elected to a post on the Macomb County Board of Commissioners.

## Gallagher, Harry (d: 1982)

Gallagher worked as an anchor and reporter at Channel 2 for four years before his death in 1982.

During his years in Detroit (1979-1982), Gallagher co-anchored Channel 2 newscasts with, variously, Joe Glover and Beverly Payne (d: 1999). Gallagher was noticeably allergic to the show-biz side of news, earning considerable respect in his short time in Detroit as a tough, forthright newsman. A former Marine, he once quit a TV news job in the Midwest and fled to a tiny station in Nome, Alaska. "He just got fed up with the show business aspects of TV News," former Channel 4 reporter Bob Vito told *Detroit Free Press* columnist Mike Duffy.

He died from cancer at age 44.

## Glover, Joe

Glover did two tours of duty as Channel 2's lead anchorman—from 1974 until 1983, and again from 1988 until 1993. Although thoroughly professional, competent and smooth, he never quite achieved the celebrity that surrounded contemporaries Bill Bonds and Mort Crim. "I really thought that I at least tried not to cave in to the tendency of television news to lean towards show biz. I tried to be a journalist rather than a television personality," he recalls.

Glover grew up in Washington, D.C., during World War II and in New England. He learned the craft in Seoul, Korea, where he broadcast news for U.S. troops who remained after the end of the Korean War. Glover's early broadcast career is testimony to the gypsy life of a news broadcaster—Miami, Miami Beach, Jacksonville, Seoul, West Palm Beach, New York City, New Orleans, San Francisco and Sacramento. His first stint at Channel 2, from 1974 until 1983, was journalistically sound but unspectacular in the way of ratings. Channel 2 General Manager Bill Flynn, who overhauled the entire news operation by way of pink slips, canned him. Glover relocated to Salinas, California, where he would have happily stayed had ownership of Channel 2 not changed. Businessman George Gillett bought the Salinas station where Glover worked, and also took ownership of Channel 2. So Glover was "transferred," even moving back into the Beverly Hills home where he had lived the first time around at Channel 2. "It was eerie," Glover recalls.

Joe Glover did several tours of duty at Channel 2, plus a brief stint at Channel 50.

The second time around was pretty much like the first: Glover serving up journalism, and nothing wild to note—except for the time when he was suspended for throwing a chair at his boss. He left the business in 1993 and went scuba diving for two years. "I think I saw the same change in Detroit that was taking place everywhere: a slide into more commercialism, a slide into show biz, a diminution of journalistic value. When I first got to Detroit, even back then, people were still thinking of names like Murrow and Sevareid and real journalism." Glover went back to school and earned a Ph.D. in mass communications at the University of Florida, where he now teaches.

## Gordon, Lou (d: 1977)

There was no public affairs show on Detroit television that even remotely resembled Lou Gordon's Channel 50 interview program, which aired from 1965 until Gordon's death in 1977 from a heart attack. Nor has there been one since.

No politician or company was too big to escape Gordon's persistent wrath. During his broadcasting career, he didn't go after the little guys. He went after mayors, governors and large industrial corporations whom he felt abused the public's trust. He clashed with Detroit Mayors Louis Miriani and Jerome P. Cavanagh. Michigan Governor George Romney walked off his show. Michigan Bell (now SBC Ameritech) and General Motors Corporation were also targets.

A Detroit native, Gordon started out his professional career after World War II working for Drew Pearson—the most feared muckraker of his day—on his newspaper column. Gordon would have stayed there, but returned to Detroit during the early 1950s to run the family business after his father had a stroke. Gordon's day job for years was as a local middleman for a women's clothing manufacturer. His real love was political commentary, first on Channel 7 (where he hosted *Lou Gordon's Hotseat*), later on WXYZ-AM,

Lou Gordon (right) in mid confrontation.

and eventually Channel 50. During the late 1960s, he even co-founded his own magazine, *Scope,* with journalist Jim Dygert. The magazine did well until the end of the 1967-1968 Detroit newspaper strike, after which it folded. *Scope,* like Gordon's broadcasts, had an angry feel about it.

But there was a lot more to Gordon. He was Detroit's Mike Wallace, a broadcast cop who cowered before no one. The bigger the interview, the tougher he got. Most interviewers bowed and scraped before Bob Hope, but Gordon asked him about his defense of President Richard Nixon during the Vietnam era. Gordon questioned George Wallace's sanity—to his face. Gordon was, by far, the most feared man in television—maybe in the history of the local medium. And no other Detroit television program ever dealt with serious issues in such a detailed manner.

It was on Gordon's show in 1967 that Michigan Governor George Romney, at the time a serious presidential candidate, said he had been "brainwashed" on the topic of Vietnam. Romney was roundly ridiculed for using the word, and forced out of the presidential race, which was later won by Richard Nixon. Gordon also accused Detroit Mayor Louis Miriani of funny stuff with campaign contributions. Miriani later spent time in jail for tax evasion involving—what else?—campaign contributions. Such accusations always made his bosses nervous, but Gordon always assured them that he had facts to back them up.

Mostly, Gordon made for riveting television. He'd field questions from viewers, as read by his wife, Jackie (d: 1999), who became as famous as her husband. He had a way of connecting directly with the viewer, something that Bill Bonds became famous for. He'd go after unobvious targets, such as Michigan Bell, which always seemed to be raising its rates. Gordon would read the fine print of the company's annual report, find some outrageous nugget that the company would rather not have anybody notice and rail about it on television. Nowadays, most TV reporters would ignore such a story

**Channel 50's Lou Gordon often clashed with Michigan Governor George Romney. But once, in 1973, Romney walked off of Gordon's show. Here's how it went:**

**Gordon**: You're still an idealist, aren't you?

**Romney**: I can't go on and give examples of…

**Gordon**: But, you're still an idealist, aren't you?

**Romney**: Well, sure I'm an idealist, but on the other hand I'm a practical idealist, because we've been doing things in this area, in this country, that you haven't given me time to talk about, such as Dayton, Ohio, where they have a fair share plan, and Washington, D.C., the great Washington, D.C., area, where they've dealt with this problem and are providing this freedom of movement, and so on, for people regardless, and getting rid of these barriers, see. So there's some patterns developing, but anyway, Lou, you haven't changed either. (Gordon laughs). You throw all the dirt you can, in as short a time as you can, and all of the misquotes and everything. And then you expect a fellow to sit here and undertake to answer all of it in just two or three minutes. And it's impossible.

**Gordon**: Well, now, what kind of dirt did I throw at you—and misquotes, governor?

**Romney**: Well, you pick out every little critical thing that's been said and then you expect me to sit here in a few minutes and try and answer it. And it's impossible.

**Gordon**: Governor, I didn't pick out every critical thing that's been said…

**Romney**: Almost every one, almost everything that's been said in the last few years of a critical character with respect to me, you've thrown at me here today.

**Gordon**: You think I've really thrown at you, all of the critical things that have been said about you?

**Romney**: Sure, sure, yes sir.

**Gordon**: Governor, now there's so many things, I mean … I … I, well obviously if you think that, I'm not going to change your mind, but I … I.

**Romney**: Well, you're still doing the same thing. I thought maybe you'd be interested in what I'm going to do. I thought maybe you'd have some sort of interest in things other than just every critical aspect.

**Gordon**: Let's stop for a moment. Let's go another segment, and let's find out what you're going to do.

**Romney**: I thought maybe you'd be interested in what I've done, but you don't do that.

**Gordon**: Can't we go another segment? Let's take another segment and go.

**Romney**: Ahh. (Throws mike down)

**Gordon**: Don't you want to take another segment? No?

**Romney**: Goodbye, goodbye. (He walks away, but returns toward Gordon, shaking his finger) … with the negative and you go just as negative as you can all the way through …

**Gordon**: I'm sorry you feel that way.

because there was no tape (or video) to go with it. To abuse the famous line from *The Treasure of the Sierra Madre*, Gordon didn't need no stinkin' video. He'd be so engrossed with a topic that it would never occur to him that the subject was impossibly complicated or dull. Since he was so engrossed, he never came off as dull—no matter what the topic. And he didn't need a set, or at least not much of one. Gordon's TV surroundings involved a desk and a couple of chairs—nothing more.

There was much debate about Gordon's accuracy. Although Gordon was never successfully sued for libel, one can come up with examples where he was less than complete in telling a story. During one tirade, he accused Ma Bell of having more employees making more than $40,000 per year than the other three major utilities combined. True, the phone company said. But the company also had 5,000 more employees than the other three utilities combined.

Such oversights made him something of a pariah in traditional journalism circles. Professional journalists often hated him because he never trained in a newsroom. However, Gordon pursued straight journalism's most revered mission—to comfort the afflicted and afflict the comfortable. To him, the words meant something. He wasn't anybody's lap dog. *Detroit News* columnist Pete Waldmeir wondered aloud after Gordon's death if journalists were envious of Gordon's power. "A lot of people in Detroit's mass media were jealous of Lou's success," Waldmeir wrote after Gordon died in his sleep. "I'm not certain that, deep down, I wasn't one of them."

Nobody carried on in his place. Channel 50 hired Barry Farber, a New York City radio host, to carry on after Gordon was buried, but quickly cancelled. And who in the TV medium goes after targets such as Ameritech?

Nobody, unfortunately.

## Grant, Austin

Grant anchored Channel 9s newscasts in the 1950s. With his thin mustache, precise diction and old-school manners, he looked like an officer in the British Royal Air Force. In fact, he was a radio veteran who moved into TV during the medium's infancy.

The newscaster grew up in Ohio and studied drama in both New York and Boston. He made use of the experience by pro-

Channel 9's Austin Grant.

ducing dramatic and musical shows on Broadway. His first job in Detroit broadcasting was at WWJ-AM, in 1937. After a stop at WXYZ-AM, he became Channel 9's news director, leading both the radio and TV news departments. His sign-off phrase, "That'll be all … from Austin Grant," was his trademark. An ardent antique collector and expert on homes, he also hosted Channel 9's *Home Fair*.

In 1965, when the station's management wanted to split the radio and TV operations, Grant objected, pointing out that there wasn't enough money to support two news departments and that the management would get two lousy news operations instead of one good one. He was fired. A bit of trivia: Grant was a member of the Livonia City Council.

## Gray, Solon

He was brought in to replace Bill Bonds, when Bonds left for Los Angeles in the late 1960s. Channel 7's front office teamed him up with Barney Morris, who was Bonds' former partner, thinking a Gray/Morris partnership would work as well as the Bonds/Morris duo. It didn't. He's now working at a Miami all-news radio station.

## Haney, Don

Haney held forth on Channel 7 during the 1960s and 1970s with *Haney's People*, one of the more literate and challenging talk shows in the history of Detroit television.

Haney's career illustrates the difficulties of racism in Detroit broadcasting during the 1950s. As a Northern High School student during the '50s, Haney had dreams of becoming a local broadcaster. At the time, however, one of the few places African-Americans could be heard on air was at WJLB-AM. And even then, the broadcasters heard on the station weren't full-time station employees. The station simply rented time out and left it to the broadcasters to

Vice President Hubert Humphrey visits with Don Haney.

115

fill it as profitably as they knew how. Haney knew what he was up against, but plunged on. He visited Channel 4 one day, and was told by a manager: "You're a damned fool for trying to get a job at a white station." Instead of deterring Haney it gave him the fuel to continue—and thrive—in the business.

Unable to get work in Michigan, Haney became an exile, spending most of his early career in Canada. At various times, he could be heard in Kitchener, London and St. Thomas, Ontario. Some of his work was seen and heard coast-to-coast in Canada, via the Canadian Broadcasting Co. His father, who owned the Mack Haney Funeral Home on Detroit's east side, convinced Haney to come home and perhaps run the family business. He did return, but instead landed at WJR-AM in 1964, and from there moved on to Channel 7 in late 1967.

*Haney's People* aired Sunday nights between 1967 and 1981. It would start at 11:30 p.m. and stop whenever Haney got tired—meaning the show would sometimes continue until 1 a.m., or later. He also worked on the station's news broadcasts.

Perhaps his biggest contribution to broadcasting occurred in 1969. One of the biggest news events of 1969 was the New Bethel incident. Detroit police and members of the Republic of New Africa fought a gun battle outside New Bethel Baptist Church, a major African-American institution. One Detroit policeman was killed. Several hundred people were arrested—pretty much anybody in or around the meeting at the church. But Detroit Recorder's Court Judge George Crockett Jr. released dozens on constitutional grounds. The white community was outraged. Many, without having met Crockett, thought of him as somebody from one of the many black radical movements of the time. Haney got the sole interview with Crockett and viewers saw a soft-spoken, elderly gentleman with a concern for the U.S. Constitution. It was one of the few times Crockett ever went before a television camera. After Haney's report, tension about the incident subsided somewhat.

## Hansen, Chris

This Detroit native went on to work at NBC News as a correspondent on *Dateline NBC*.

A Birmingham native and a 1981 graduate of Michigan State University, Hansen joined Channel 7 as a newsman after learning his craft in Tampa, Florida, and Lansing.

He quickly developed a reputation as a hard-charging, story-breaking journalist who was a master at developing and maintaining sources. The telling thing about Hansen was that he got along well with print reporters, cops and FBI agents, and was known as a tireless worker. Anybody who was envious of his good looks was soon disarmed by his honest charm.

Hansen's biggest booster at Channel 7 was Bill Bonds, who told Hansen that he had the talent and energy to inherit Bonds' anchor seat. When Channel 4 outbid Channel 7 for Hansen's services in early 1988, Bonds offered to give up part of his considerable salary to keep Hansen at Channel 7. The station management declined Bonds' offer. He worked at Channel 4 until 1993, when he joined NBC News. He was the first Detroit TV newsman in more than a decade to go network.

## Harlan, Carmen

Carmen Harlan's longevity has secured her place among the Motor City's video icons. A graduate of Mumford High School and the University of Michigan, she joined Channel 4 in 1978 after working as a newsreader at WWWW-FM. Post-Newsweek officials singled her out as a prospective anchor, grooming her for the chair next to Mort Crim. Harlan and Crim became one of the most successful teams in Detroit television history. Now that Crim has retired, Harlan and relative newcomer Devin Scillian still top the ratings at 11 p.m.

As of this writing, Harlan is the station's public face. She anchors the annual fireworks coverage and is the station's chief ambassador. She hosted Detroit Mayor Kwame Kilpatrick's swearing-in ceremony in 2002. Her participation brought questions from journalists who wondered about the propriety of an anchorwoman gadding about with the same politicians she is supposed to report about without fear or favor.

So what's the secret of her success? She rarely flubs a sentence, performing her job with impressive poise. Her background as a Detroiter in the highly transient broadcast business helps, too.

## Herrington, Jim

Channel 7's top political reporter for some three decades, Herrington joined the station in 1965, making a name for himself two years later with his intrepid coverage of the 1967 Detroit riots. While many TV newsmen were talking to "official" Detroit at City Hall and police headquarters, Herrington was out in the street talking to rioters. One classic moment involved a woman coming out of a store on Woodward Avenue carrying a slip. "I just needed a couple of things," she told Herrington. "Are you going to take that?" he asked. "They're gonna burn it down anyhow," she told him.

He went on to become the news department's premier point man in politics. Herrington covered some 16 Republican and Democratic conventions, interviewed every president back to Harry S Truman and was on a first-name basis with every congressman and governor anybody ever heard of. More important, he was friendly with backroom politicians that nobody ever heard of, but who knew where the bodies were buried. His casual style masked a canny political brain.

By the time of his retirement in 1993, he had become sick of TV avoiding the big political stories.

## Joyce, Andrea

This CBS Sports anchor worked at Channel 4 during the 1980s

Channel 7's Jim Herrington.

as a reporter and weekend anchor. A bundle of energy and talent, most insiders believe she would have been the station's top anchor if she had stayed.

A native of Dearborn, Joyce graduated from the University of Michigan with a speech/communications degree in 1976. After training in Wichita, Kansas, and Colorado Springs, Colorado, she joined Channel 4 in 1980. Versatility made her an important member of the staff. If the programming department needed somebody to host an event—somebody they could trust to improvise for five minutes at a time if something went wrong in the control room— Joyce got the call. If the news department needed somebody to cover a difficult story, Joyce got the call. She left the station in 1983 for Dallas, and joined CBS Sports two years later.

During her CBS Sports career, she has hosted everything from the NCAA Division I Men's Basketball Championship to the CBS coverage of the 1992 Olympic Games. She is married to Harry Smith, a *CBS This Morning* anchor she met while in Denver.

## Kelly, John

John Kelly's career covered some three decades, during which he was a successful newscaster at two television stations (Channels 2 and 7) and a successful talk show host on one (Channel 7). One of the more interesting "what ifs" in Detroit television history is this: What would have happened if Kelly had stuck with news?

A native of St. Louis and a veteran of the U.S. Navy, Kelly broke into journalism as a reporter at the *Hannibal Courier-Post.* He abandoned print rather quickly, however, and broke into television as a program director at a television station in Rockford, Illinois. Kelly worked at television stations in Lansing, Atlanta and Peoria before attracting the attention of Channel 2's Bob McBride in 1965. Kelly wrote and edited much of the newscast content and worked as a street reporter. And Kelly was serious

John Kelly's career spanned three decades at two stations—Channels 2 and 7.

119

about it, developing sources and doing his homework. The combination of Kelly, Jac Le Goff and Jerry Hodak became, in the words of Detroit attorney Henry Baskin, the "New York Yankees" of local TV. The group challenged Channel 4's news dominance. But in the end, he wrote about his news career: "I knew one thing—I had to get out! I didn't know where or to what. I just couldn't stay and do what I had been doing. It was too much. I was burned out."

"Getting out" eventually meant going to Channel 7, where he joined the "We Got Who You Wanted" collection of newscasters. Although successful, the station's management had other ideas about Kelly continuing on as a news anchor. Channel 7 General Manager Jeanne Findlater had thoughts of moving Diana Lewis or Doris Biscoe further up into the news rotation. So Kelly worked the last 20 years of his career as a talk show host.

Kelly was known as the guy who laughed a lot during the newscasts. But interviews with those who worked the newscasts during those days reveal that Kelly wasn't yukking it up as nearly as often as newscasters do these days. By the year 2003, newscasts had turned into laugh riots. Reading *Good Morning Detroit*, which is partly Kelly's autobiography, one could conclude that he was a lot closer to Walter Cronkite than Regis Philbin.

## Knight, Kirk (d: 1980)

He was everywhere on radio and television during the 1950s and 1960s—particularly in the morning. Knight did local "cut-ins"—news from Detroit—for the *Today* show (1952-1973), broadcast *Farm Report* and *Business Briefs* on WWJ-radio, and anchored Channel 4's *Country Living* program during the weekend. But Knight had other duties, too. He covered Detroit Common Council during the 1950s and 1960s, distinguishing himself as a reporter who could get information out of City Hall insiders.

Channel 4's Kirk Knight in the hunt for news.

Knight's television career didn't begin until he was 40. His video career couldn't have begun any earlier because the medium didn't exist before then. A native of Ypsilanti, Knight began his broadcasting career at WJBK-AM while still in his early twenties. Knight stayed in radio between 1929 and 1946. As Knight once told *The Detroit News'* Frank Judge, the pay for one of his depression-era radio jobs was "$5 in cash, a restaurant meal ticket and a bushel of potatoes." Channel 4 hired Knight within a month of going on the air—which makes Knight one of local TV's true pioneers.

Knight had a soft, pleasant baritone that conveyed authority without being overbearing. His soft voice made him perfect for the morning radio and TV audience, because he didn't jar anybody awake. His silver hair would remind a later generation of Ted Baxter, the goofy anchorman on *The Mary Tyler Moore Show.* The difference between Knight and Baxter was that Knight actually knew something. His gift to later generations was that he met reporter Bob Bennett while covering City Hall, and urged his supervisors at Channel 4 to hire Bennett. They did. Knight retired from Channel 4 in 1973, and died in 1980.

## Le Goff, Jac

One could argue that Jac Le Goff—not Bill Bonds—was the most important anchorman ever to work in local TV news. Le Goff appeared on three stations—Channels 2, 7 and 4—during his 35-year career. (He also worked at Channel 9 between 1960 and 1962, but that was considered only a brief period of international exile.) Channel 2 was Detroit's No. 1-rated station during the late 1960s and early 1970s with Le Goff as the lead anchor. When he left for Channel 7 in 1975, that station jumped to No. 1. It should be noted that Channel 7's leap to the top wasn't accomplished until after Le Goff signed on. Channel 7 didn't pull off that feat with only Bonds on the premises. After Le Goff's retire-

Jac Le Goff worked at all three Detroit networks, plus a stint at Channel 9.

121

**The rock radio payola scandal was in high gear when Jac Le Goff editorialized on the topic November 18, 1959. It got him fired from Channel 2. Here are excerpts of the editorial:**

"WJBK has received a number of calls from listeners today asking why we didn't carry the story concerning the disc jockeys of radio and the story about payola, or bribery, to play a certain record.

"I didn't use the story at 11 last night, realized that the newspapers would hop on this as they did on the so-called TV quiz payoffs. This sort of newspaper sensationalism can be handled by those who are not in the business, apparently.

"But are their skirts as clean as they would like you to believe? What about the Bob Considine story of alleged payola and the same type story of two other well-known columnists? They were buried in the back pages by those who employ them. Payola has been known to exist in the industry for many months. Those who deny they have ever been approached to take payola are perhaps employees of smaller stations in smaller markets ...

"What about the buyers in department stores, in grocery stories—'buy one case of my product and you get one free; you buy my blue jeans by the gross ... and I'll remember you at Christmas time.' Is this not payola? Have there not been other accusations of this same sort in the federal government, in the Federal Communications Commission, in the garment industry? Payola in one form or another is a part of American business.

"This is certainly not to say that I or the broadcasting industry condones the practice, but I say, 'Let him who is without sin cast the first stone.'"

ment from Channel 7, he joined Channel 4 in 1985 as editorial director. When some smart person decided to have Le Goff anchor the station 5 p.m. newscast at Channel 4, the newscast shot to No. 1—something Channel 4 had been unable to pull off before. He never added unnecessary drama or silliness to the news. He delivered the news straight. And he had a sense of humor, both on camera and off.

Le Goff first became interested in broadcasting as a Navy man, delivering reports to fellow sailors. He joined Channel 2 in 1953 as a booth announcer and was successful there as an anchorman until being canned in late 1959 for editorializing about a payola scandal in the radio business. (Channel 2 was owned by Storer Broadcasting, as was WJBK-AM, a popular rock radio station that employed several deejays implicated in the scandal.) "Everybody in the building knew what was going on," he recalled later. "I had proof of everything I commented on." However, Le Goff's editorial cost him his job within 24 hours. He spent a two-year hiatus at Channel 9, until being rehired by Channel 2 in 1962.

It was in the late 1960s that Le Goff's career really took off. He was teamed with John Kelly, and the team appeared to have the same chemistry as NBC's popular combination of Chet Huntley and David Brinkley. Le Goff's direct style of delivery meshed well with Kelly's lighter touch. The two were said to have brought "Happy Talk" to the Detroit television audience, but Le Goff bristles at the suggestion. For instance, he points out that he and Kelly joked only on occasion—compared to the current-day anchors, who look like they're auditioning for a job at Comedy Castle.

Le Goff was the first Detroit anchor ever to break the "$1 million dollar" mark—he signed a contract in 1975 that gave him the money during a seven-year period. That was front-page news at the time.

He once appeared in an ABC Warehouse ad in which a boy walks into the store and says to Jac: "Hi, Mr. Bonds." The youngster's embarrassed father says: "Sorry, Mort."

## Makeupson, Amyre

She was Channel 50's lead journalist, and the only employee to last throughout the life of the station's 10 p.m. newscast. She joined the station in 1977 as news and public affairs manager, just as the 10 o'clock news debuted; and she was there December 2, 2002, when the newscast signed off for the last time, a victim of poor ratings and CBS's lack of commitment to journalism.

Makupson grew up in Detroit and attended Fisk University in Nashville. Her early years in journalism say something about her dedication to her craft. Makupson had been working for $22,000 a year in public relations, but took a $10,000 pay cut to work for WGPR-TV's *Big City News*. When the station ran into financial difficulties, she worked at WGPR-TV for free. When invited to work at Channel 50, she recalls being somewhat reluctant about getting into the uncertain world of broadcasting.

In her 25 years there she was serious about the news, and about community—and it showed. Even after leaving Channel 50, she still held positions on a half-dozen boards and committees.

## Marlin-Jones, Davey (d: 2004)

One of the most distinctive voices ever to work in local television, Jones reviewed movies on Channel 4 between September 1978 and April 1986. But it wasn't the movie reviews that made Jones distinctive. It was his presentation: He dressed in a cape and unusual hat, did card tricks during and after his reviews, and served up his observations in a droll, poetic fashion spoken in a cadence not heard before—or since.

Jones was not, primarily, a television guy. His education and area of expertise was theatre. (As a young man, Jones had made one stop in Detroit. Traveling from his native Winchester, Indiana, to New York City, he paused in Detroit for what he thought would be a few days while he made a few bucks on the way to the East Coast. He stayed for three years, 1955-1958, working in advertising.) He made it to New York, and then on to Washington, D.C. Years later, Jones was teaching a theatre class in Washington D.C., when a Post-Newsweek Station executive petitioned Jones to try out for the drama critic's job. By then, his resume included senior positions at the Kennedy Center, where he ran the New Playwrights program. His career also included work in Cincinnati and St. Louis.

Initially, he was brought to town by Post-Newsweek after the station bought Channel 4 in 1978. The thinking was that Jones would signal a different direction for the station. That he did splendidly, splitting his time between Detroit and the former Post-Newsweek outlet in Washington, D.C. But he was a bit too unusual for the meat-and-potatoes Detroit TV crowd, so he was gone within a few years. "I'd fly to Detroit about every two weeks. The top guy at the station in Detroit wasn't crazy about my work. And he wasn't necessarily in a minority," Jones later recounted in an interview. "The rap was that I couldn't talk to regular folks." That would have been hard to prove the day Jones and his wife showed up at Tiger Stadium to catch a game. The crowd chanted, "Davey, Davey, Davey."

He taught at the University of Las Vegas, where he got the appreciation he seemingly missed in Detroit. Jones received the university's Outstanding Teacher Award at UNLV's School of Fine and Performing Arts in 1998.

Channel 4's Davey Marlin-Jones.

## McNew, Leon

He was Channel 7's first anchorman, Bill Bonds' predecessor, and a walking illustration of why the TV business is not for the faint of heart.

There is nothing in McNew's background, other than plenty of experience as an announcer and prematurely white hair, to qualify him for life in the newsroom. He was "Captain Flint," for which he introduced western movies. Viewers would be hard-pressed to identify McNew, because he wore a mask. Other duties at the station included serving as a pit reporter for Fred Wolf at Motor City Speedway and as the announcer for Edythe Fern Melrose, a.k.a.: the Lady of Charm.

The Lady of Charm's send-off for McNew was less than charming, according to Dick Osgood's retelling. "Ladies, it's my displeasure to have to tell you that my right arm is not going to be with me any more. The announcer we all loved so long is leaving us to become a newscaster right here on Channel 7. I'm sure you all join me in wishing him the best of success. So let's all say good-bye to my dear friend—Lee … uh … Lee New."

According to Osgood, McNew just happened by as anchor auditions were being held. Dick Femmel, the Channel 7 official running the audition, conceded that McNew "looked good." Osgood's comment: "His face wore a natural expression of relaxed vigor, his white hair gave an impression of authority and he was not pompous."

In that way, McNew resembled classic British "newsreaders" who are hired more for their style than for their journalistic knowledge. McNew lasted several years, and was replaced by Bill Bonds. Ted Shaker, the president of ABC-owned stations, told McNew at a Channel 7 party that everything was great. The next day, Shaker ordered McNew fired.

## MacGregor, Byron (d: 1995)

Detroit radio news's most distinctive voice of the 1970s and 1980s was also the first Channel 50 10 p.m. news anchor. MacGregor (real name: Gary Mack) became famous during the late 1960s as an integral part of the CKLW-AM 20/20 news team.

Heard at 20 minutes before and 20 minutes after each hour, the CK style was saturated with shocking and/or titillating news items. One famous example cited in the book, *Rockin' Down the Dial*, had a newsreader kicking off a newscast with a headline: "Bodies, bodies, three bags full."

MacGregor was among the wildest of them all and rose to the position of news director at the station at the age of 21— the youngest person to ever hold such a position at a major market radio station. Soon after the release of his spoken-word record, "The Americans," MacGregor became an international sensation. His 1976 wedding to Jo-Jo Shutty, CKLW-AM's traffic reporter, was a media event. When he joined all-news WWJ-AM, he toned himself down. And when he began anchoring Channel 50's newscast, he toned himself down even further. But he still had that magnificent voice. And for a while he had two simultaneous gigs: afternoon newsman on WWJ-AM and the 10 o'clock anchor at Channel 50.

During the 1980s, MacGregor's luck ran out. He was relieved of his duties at WWJ-AM. It left MacGregor scrambling for work at the time of his death, from pneumonia, in early 1995.

Channel 50's Byron MacGregor.

## Marshall, S.L.A. (d: 1977)

"Slam" Marshall is the only person in the history of Detroit television news who could heave a grenade almost 75 yards. That fact alone would qualify him for the job he held, which was Channel 4's military analyst during the 1960s and early 1970s. But there were other things that qualified him for the post: He fought in World War I while still in his teens, wrote 30 books, including *Pork Chop Hill*, which was made into a film starring Gregory Peck, and penned numerous studies for countless military publications. All of that gained him a few detractors. Colonel David Hackworth once referred to Marshall as the "Louella Parsons of the battlefield." Marshall's eye patch, which he wore

Channel 4's S.L.A. Marshall.

on camera, gave him the look of a character from *Dr. Strangelove*. During the 1960s, his show was seen weekly at 6:15 p.m. Saturdays.

A native of New York, Samuel Lyman Atwood Marshall moved to Texas as a youngster and appeared in the old Bronco Billy horse shows in the southwest. Marshall enlisted in the Army just prior to the outbreak of World War I. While still only 17 years of age, Marshall was promoted to second lieutenant. His *Detroit News* obituary said he was the youngest officer in the Army during that war, although that claim is open to question. Also, he once hurled a grenade 73 yards and 26 inches during a contest. Military authorities, based on Marshall's astonishing technique, later rewrote the book on how to chuck the lethal explosive.

During his 50-year professional career, Marshall shuffled between newspaper work and the military. He worked as a soldier during World War II, the Korean conflict and the Sinai War of 1956. When Marshall wasn't soldiering, he wrote editorials and military analysis for *The Detroit News*. He also provided coverage of the Spanish Civil War.

But it wasn't until the late 1960s, after he had retired from both *The News* and the military, that Marshall became something of a local television star. He appeared often on Channel 4 during the late 1960s to dissect the Vietnam War. He was eventually fired because—as Marshall's colleagues believed—his hawkish views on the Vietnam War drove viewers away. "The general mood of the public was anti-Vietnam," remembered Jim Clark, one of Marshall's friends and a former boss. "Sam was very pro-Vietnam. This was showing up in ratings, because people didn't want to turn on with this war hawk. … (Viewers) didn't want to be preached at." Marshall sued, but settled out of court with Channel 4. He died in 1977 in Texas.

Marshall's 2,237-volume library was donated to the University of Texas-El Paso. The library's collection also includes 122 boxes of Marshall's notes and one box of his medals.

A dozen years after his death, two historians and a writer charged that Marshall's 1947 book, *Men Against Fire*, was a fraud. In that book, Marshall claimed that when a commander goes into battle "not more than one quarter of his men will ever strike a real blow." Marshall based that belief on interviews with hundreds upon hundreds of soldiers immediately after battle. But two historians—one from Sarah Lawrence College, the other from the Army's Command and General Staff College—claimed that Marshall made up the evidence. Marshall's estranged grandson, who missed the Vietnam War as a conscientious objector, defended his grandfather.

## Marshall, Ven (d: 1989)

Marshall, who worked at Channels 4 and 7 from the mid-1950s to 1987, covered virtually every major political and labor event in Detroit between the 1950s and 1980s. Peers considered him among the best newsmen who ever worked a microphone. He spent hours cultivating sources, most of whom would then become willing to help Marshall when big stories broke. "If he had been covering the Titanic," Bill Bonds once remarked, "he would have had a guy on the iceberg with a cell phone waiting to call Ven when it happened." When covering labor stories, it probably helped that his brother was Bill Marshall, longtime head of metro Detroit's AFL-CIO.

A smallish man with a dramatic baritone, he worked at radio stations in Flint and Louisiana before he was hired by WWJ-TV (now WDIV) in 1956. "Ven had a vinyl disc recording of his work during the (1956) Flint tornado," recalled former Channel 4 news director Jim Clark. "He did really outstanding work." Marshall spent 12 years at Channel 4, and was one of the station's most important figures. "When he worked, he was intense—a buzz saw," recalls Dwayne X. Riley. "In those days, when he was

Newsman Ven Marshall in the 1950s.

**Mary Conway was a young reporter at Channel 7, and was undergoing the usual difficulties of working as a rookie in a major market television newsroom. The late Ven Marshall helped make Conway's life easier—and taught her a few lessons about journalism, too.**

"When I started, he was quite a bit older. And a lot of the (older) people had a real chip on their shoulders about the new people coming in. But he was wonderful to me, and always took time to help me. When I would come down and be like the second person on a story, such as the auto talks, he was wonderful about introducing me to (United Auto Workers President) Owen Bieber. He was fabulous in how he treated the new people. We were all part of the same team. And a lot of times people aren't like that. ...

"I learned a lot from Ven: To ask the tough questions and to listen. That's something we're always supposed to do, but Ven was a master of knowing that what was important was what they *weren't* saying. When they would come out and make some big announcement ... he was very good about reading between the lines. When they would announce that somebody had been elevated to a certain position, it meant that somebody else had been fired or pushed aside. People to this day don't seem to realize that. When they announce the new president of a certain division of one of the Big Three, it usually means the other guy has been forced out. ...The devil was in the details, in paying attention to what they were saying."

anchoring the news on weekends, it was a simple operation. There would be one crew—and that would be it. They didn't go out unless something really big happened. We didn't have producer upon producer, assistant producers, writers and the rest. He would do it all. He'd mat these photographs, run across the room to answer the telephone, write something, and run back to the photo machine for more photographs. It was amazing to see. All of it was way beyond the call of duty. But that was Ven—extraordinarily conscientious."

In addition to being a buzz saw, Marshall was also a character. He always introduced himself: "I'm Vendex Faust Marshall Junior from Tunica, Mississippi—the poorest town in the poorest county in the poorest state of the United States."

Marshall lost his job with Channel 4 in 1968. His career was supposed to be over, but Channel 7 hired him within days and made him one of their stars. Phil Nye, the station's news director, gave everybody "beats." Marshall's beat was the UAW and the auto companies. At one point in the early 1980s, Marshall was believed to be the highest-paid street reporter in Detroit. He died after a long illness in 1989 at his vacation retreat in the Dominican Republic.

## Miller, Dean (d: 2004)

Miller was Channel 4's anchor after the station's early glory days with Dick Westerkamp and before the advent of Mort Crim. Before joining Channel 4 in 1972, Miller spent his career bouncing between journalism and Hollywood. He hosted a morning show, *There's One In Every Family* in the early 1950s, played Matt Henshaw on CBS's *December Bride* between 1954 and 1961, bought a few radio stations and a weekly newspaper in Ohio, decided to get back into anchoring and established himself as a newsman in Miami—which is where Channel 4 executives found him.

They thought they had the perfect antidote to Channel 7's Bill

Channel 4's Dean Miller.

Bonds, who was coming on strong. They thought Miller's low-key style would be a welcome contrast to Bonds' flamboyance. They were wrong. Although the ratings were OK, Miller lost his job in 1975 because of "demographics"—meaning not enough young people were watching his newscasts. Post-TV, Miller sold insurance in Grosse Pointe. His daughter, Toni, developed into a respected radio newswoman on WWWW-FM during the 1990s.

## Moore, Jennifer

Channel 4's Jennifer Moore might have been the best-informed and most able broadcast reporters to cover business during the 1990s. Her business reports on the station's early evening newscasts were informed, accurate and loaded with insight. Most TV reporters, stressed and running from story to story because they're required to churn out three reports or more a day, no longer have the time for the type of homework Moore routinely did.

Moore grew up in Ohio, coming to Detroit in 1975 as a reporter for WJR-AM, where she impressed everybody with her energy and unflappability. Channel 4 hired her as a street reporter, even pairing her with Mort Crim briefly on the anchor desk during the 1980s. She is now in the media training business with Beth Konrad, a former Channel 4 colleague.

## Morris, Barney (d: 2003)

He was one of the first two on-air reporters hired in 1964 as Channel 7 seriously began building its news operation. (The other reporter was Bill Bonds, Morris' friend and former WKNR-AM colleague.)

A graduate of the University of Detroit, Morris worked radio in the 1950s, once working as a deejay at a station in Monroe under the name "Glen Howard." He later became news director at WCAR-AM during the early 1960s. One of his employees was a young Bill Bonds. "The station owner came in one day and wanted me to fire pretty much the entire news department. I thought everybody was doing a good job, including Bill, and wouldn't do it. So the owner fired me." He ended up at WJBK-AM as a newsman, and eventually went across the hall to Channel 2 (WJBK-TV, which shared the same owner as the radio station) as a part-time sportscaster subbing for Bill Flemming.

Channel 7 stole Morris away in 1964. The station started a two-hour color newscast, a big move in those days and needed credible, productive reporters to fill the time and mold themselves into a team. By the time the 1967 riots erupted, Morris, Bonds, and reporters Ken Thomas and Jim Herrington were, indeed, a team as they turned in the journalistic performances of their lives. Channel 7's coverage gained critical notice. It also earned promotions for almost everybody involved: Bonds, news director Bill Fyffe and Morris all ended up in Los Angeles during the late 1960s.

The rest of Morris's career was successful. He anchored in Los Angeles, San Diego and Philadelphia before settling down as a street reporter in Los Angeles for more than a decade. "The thing about anchoring," he later recalled, "is that if you fail, you're fired. So you've got to move. If you're successful, somebody from another town hires you, so you've got to move. I'd had enough."

He retired during the late 1990s and settled in West Virginia, where he died.

## Murphy, Terry

She was at Channel 2 for less than two years in the mid-1970s, but she was a big deal when she was here. The time line: She arrived from Cincinnati in September 1974. By April 1975 she was anchoring the station's 11 p.m. newscast with Ken Thomas. By December, she announced she was leaving Channel 2 for ABC's station in Chicago. Murphy was young (27), hip and

Channel 2's Terry Murphy.

popped through the screen—and a real threat to Channel 7. She was also only the second woman in Detroit to anchor a major evening newscast. So Channel 7, through its owners at ABC in New York, arranged for a nice spot for Murphy in Chicago—where she was very successful.

She later went on to CBS and ABC-owned stations in Los Angeles before anchoring the tabloid news magazine, *Hard Copy*. She also played herself in a number of films, including *Casper*, *An Affair to Remember* and *Major League II*. More recently, she was spotted anchoring an entertainment news program on the Internet.

## Nunn, Guy (d: 1984)

He was the radio and television voice of the United Auto Workers throughout the 1950s and early 1960s, broadcasting the union's take on local issues.

Nunn grew up in Los Angeles, the son of a working class family. He went on to become a Rhodes Scholar and served in World War II as a member of the U.S. Office of Strategic Services (predecessor to the Central Intelligence Agency). In other words, he was a spy. The Nazi Gestapo took Nunn into custody in 1944 and sentenced him to death. He was freed by Allied forces in 1945.

Back home, he joined WJR-AM as a newscaster, but didn't last long. Labor historians have two theories about his firing from WJR: that he gave GM strikers fair coverage in 1946 and that he had tried to cover Richard Frankensteen's Detroit mayoral candidacy without bias. Walter Reuther hired him in 1948, and made him chief of the UAW's radio and television department, which transformed him into one of the best-known members of the UAW hierarchy.

Nunn was omnipresent: On radio, he anchored *Eye Opener* and *Shift Break*. On TV, he was seen sometimes twice daily. When the Democratic party needed somebody to debate George Romney in

UAW spokesman Guy Nunn, the working man's intellectual.

his 1962 run for governor, Nunn was chosen.

In the end, Nunn became a victim of his own fame. He was eased out "in part because his own still-radical personage had won a far higher profile in the shops than that of many regional directors," according to historian Nelson Lichtenstein's biography of Walter Reuther, *The Most Dangerous Man In Detroit: Walter Reuther and the Fate of American Labor.*

Nunn retired to Hawaii, where he died in 1984.

## Payne, Beverly (d: 1999)

Payne had a 13-year career at Channel 2, where she became the first African-American female to anchor the news in Detroit. "She was a trailblazer," said former Channel 7 anchorwoman Doris Biscoe in Payne's *Detroit Free Press* obituary. "It was a tough position to hold, and she held it with dignity and class."

Payne, who was born in San Francisco, had something of a varied career before getting into TV: She modeled and taught English in Japan before relocating to the Detroit area in the early 1970s. Channel 2 hired her as a receptionist, but put her on the air in 1973. Payne stayed for 13 years, anchoring the noon and 6 p.m. newscasts. After TV, she worked as a public relations specialist. She died from cancer in San Francisco, at the age of 54.

## Perkins, Huel

He's Channel 2's lead news anchor at the start of the new millennium. Perkins grew up in Baton Rouge, Louisiana, the son of an educator. (It is ironic that Perkins' father had applied to Louisiana State University in the 1940s, but was denied admittance because he was black. As of this writing, the elder Perkins was the assistant to the chancellor at LSU, and a very powerful man on campus.)

The younger Perkins started out wanting to become a lawyer. After graduating from Central State University in Wilberforce,

Channel 2's Beverly Payne.

Ohio, Perkins went on to study at the Southern University Law Center in Baton Rouge. While in law school, he worked part time at a radio station. It became clear that Perkins had talent for the medium. After five years there, he jumped to KSDK-TV in St. Louis, Missouri, where he worked for Mort Meisner and Steve Antoniotti. When Meisner and Antoniotti joined Channel 2, Perkins was one of their first hires.

Perkins can testify to the weirdness of the television business. He was informed in the mid-1990s that he was making too much money and that his Channel 2 contract wouldn't be renewed. Perkins immediately fielded an offer from an Atlanta television station. However, the general manager who had told Perkins he was finished in Detroit was replaced. The new general manager, Jim Clayton, told Perkins to forget what the first guy said and asked Perkins to stick around. At the same time, another Atlanta station became interested in Perkins. This meant that he went from no job to three offers, all in a three-month period. He stuck with Channel 2.

## Pisor, Bob

In terms of journalistic experience, few in Detroit television could match Channel 4's Bob Pisor. His work history included assignments as a political writer at *The Detroit News,* as editor of *Detroit Monthly* magazine, and as a press secretary to the late Mayor Coleman A. Young, to whom he became a confidante. He also wrote a book, *The End of the Line: The Siege of Khe Sanh*, which examined one of the Vietnam War's most important battles. He brought his wealth of experience to Channel 4, where he worked throughout the 1980s and into the early 1990s.

Pisor first signed on at Channel 4 as the station's media critic, where he delivered original, informed, pithy critiques of the town's two big daily newspapers. Nobody had ever done that before. He became so skilled before the camera that he soon became the station's weekend anchorman and political reporter. Most agree that his reporting during the next decade or so—particularly on political issues—was first class. However, political reporting on television became an unappreciated talent, so Pisor ended up out of the business. He sold the clothes he wore on television at a garage sale and now runs Stone House Bread, an organic bread-making concern in northern Michigan. He served one term on the Leelenau County Commission in 2001-2002 and is also writing a book about the ancient Spartan general Brasidas (d: 422 B.C.).

## Riley, Dwayne X.

Riley's career stretched from 1960 until his retirement in 1994—all at Channel 4. The 34-year tenure may be a record in Detroit TV. During those years, he did everything from anchoring the news to hosting a call-in show on radio (*Newscall*) to his wacky *Riley's World* TV news features, for which he became well known. Although Riley was perfectly capable of covering hard news (having covered labor, police beat and elections for Channel 4 during the 1960s and 1970s), his specialty was the feature. The station gave Riley five minutes of his own for features following George Pierrot's program during the 1970s. During the 1980s and 1990s, Channel 4 concluded many of its weekday newscasts with *Riley's World*, which would highlight Riley's take on the weird and quirky—such as a trained squirrel who could drive a small boat—to the serious, such as spending a week on skid row.

Riley's early career included stops at Grand Rapids, Minnesota; Mason City, Iowa; Grand Forks, North Dakota; and Stevens Point, Wisconsin. He was almost fired in Mason City for repeating on-air a phrase uttered to him by a transmitter technician. Riley called to the transmitter to ask the temperature—information he would use on the air. The techie told Riley: "When the frost is on the pump-

Channel 4's Dwayne X. Riley.

kin, it's time for peter dunkin'." Somehow, the saying's bawdiness escaped Riley. "I'd never heard the phrase before," Riley said, "so I said it on-air. The general manager exiled me to the record library for about two weeks." He also worked as a broadcaster while in the U.S. Army (1955-1957) but had to work to earn the audition. Riley had been stationed in Moji Port, Japan. The only place the U.S. Army held on-air auditions was in Yokohama. His supervisors were reluctant to let him go, but he sent two bottles of V.O. their way and promised to transport a prisoner to a detention facility in Yokohama if they'd let him go for 48 hours to the audition.

After stops in Lansing and Saginaw, Riley was hired by Channel 4 officials in 1960 to replace Carl Cederberg, who had gone to Channel 2. Riley started out anchoring a 15-minute newscast on WWJ-AM at 7 a.m., then started doing newscasts at 8 a.m., 9 a.m. and noon, as well. He produced twenty six 30-minute features on conditions at Jackson Prison and the Detroit House of Corrections in April-May 1962. Early in his career, Riley developed his original, quirky style of covering feature stories. "I'd broken all kinds of stories, but you know what people remember? The story about, say, Thanksgiving Dinner at your house." To that end, he teamed up with Lare Wardrop, an oboe player with the Detroit Symphony Orchestra who also shot film for the station. Together, they turned out clever, creative journalism that blended well with the rest of a reporting staff that included Britton Temby, Ven Marshall and George Pruette.

Riley's career included several important broadcasts: He spent a week on skid row in 1976 and did a weeklong report about the experience. To answer an oft-asked question, his middle initial stands for "Xavior."

## Sanders, Ron

Sanders was the hustling rookie reporter at Channel 2 during the 1970s. He had been working at radio in his native Jackson since age 15, and followed news executive Richard Van Wie when Van Wie moved from Jackson to Detroit. Sanders' first job, which he landed in 1971, was on the Channel 2 assignment desk. He was only 18 and still a Wayne State University student. "I did everything from running the assignment desk, to editing, writing, to picking up film at the airport," he recalled. Sanders also produced for Vic Caputo on the weekends. Within a few months, as a precocious 19-year-old, he went on the air. He eventually anchored Channel 2's *PM Magazine*.

Sanders left Detroit for a TV reporting job in Boston, where he has remained since 1979. Most recently, he has been a general assignment reporter at Boston's CBS-owned station, WBZ-TV.

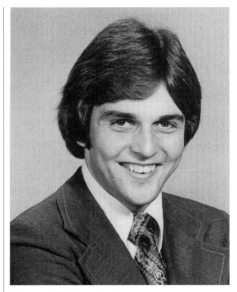
Channel 2's Ron Sanders.

## Sarginson, Wes

Sarginson anchored Channel 4's newscasts before Post-Newsweek Stations brought Mort Crim to town.

Born in Alabama, Sarginson had been anchoring the news in Washington, D.C., when Channel 4 brought him to Detroit in 1975. During his stay here, Sarginson once guest-hosted an episode of *Hee Haw*, which Channel 4 carried during the 1970s. Only 31 years old at the time of his Detroit hiring, Sarginson might have remained here if Post-Newsweek hadn't acquired the station. Sarginson quit for a job in Atlanta only weeks before the takeover took effect. As of 2004, he was still anchoring the news in Atlanta.

## Smith, Erik

Smith has done virtually everything during a career at Channel 7 that spans nearly 40 years. He currently anchors the station's early morning newscast, and has won several national awards for his finely tuned work on the station's *From The Heart* segments. At various times he has also worked as a weathercaster and feature reporter. He can handle hard-news assignments, too. At one

Channel 4's Wes Sarginson.

point during the early 1960s, when he was barely 21, he was Channel 7's news director. Of course, there wasn't much news to direct—Channel 7's news department consisted of roughly three people—but it looked good on the resume.

Smith, a native of Dearborn, attended Wayne State University and first came to Channel 7 in 1962 as a sound effects technician. He worked on wrestling shows and also with Johnny Ginger. Later, however, he hitched on with the news department, where he began as a writer. News Director Bill Fyffe, certain that Smith would become a great reporter if he had seasoning, helped get him hired. He signed on as a reporter at WKNR-AM, one of the best news operations in Detroit broadcasting (Smith's colleagues included Vince Wade, Bill Bonds and Ken Ford). Smith became assistant news director under Phil Nye.

He's had only one out-of-town stop: in the late 1960s, as a reporter/weatherman in San Francisco. Smith arrived there on a Friday afternoon, hoping to begin work on a Monday. The news director ordered him into the station immediately. The anchorman was away because of a snit, the sportscaster was upset about something else and the weatherman was drunk. Smith did all three reports—and got an unpleasant review from the late Herb Caen, the legendary *San Francisco Chronicle* columnist. "Who's the used car salesman from Cleveland on Channel 5?" Caen wanted to know. Smith left the business during the early 1970s for a brief time, working as a pitchman for the old Wrigley supermarkets. He didn't like it much, and ended up laying sod in Westland for $2 an hour. Eventually, he returned to the old Channel 7 newsroom and has enjoyed a 25-year streak of steady work.

Smith is regarded by some as the station's institutional memory.

## Spotlight On The News

Detroit television's oldest public affairs show. *Spotlight* went on the air in 1965, with Channel 7 News Director Bill Fyffe serving as host. Five years later, reporter/political analyst Jim Herrington became the host, and stayed until his retirement in 1993. Channel 7 Editorial Director Chuck Stokes took over *Spotlight* upon Herrington's retirement. Along the way, the program's guests have included two presidents (Bush and Clinton), three U.S. senators (Riegle, Levin, Abraham), numerous U.S. cabinet members and a long line of local politicos.

## Stanecki, Jerry

Stanecki was Detroit television's first "Newshawk"—a reporter who helped viewers in need; a kind of Superman with a camera crew. The beneficiaries of Stanecki's work at Channel 7 between 1976 and 1987 included a cancer-stricken Romulus youngster. Stanecki flew the youngster and his mother to Hollywood, with a limousine at the other end, where they met TV's Laverne and Shirley and the Fonz.

Stanecki started his Detroit broadcasting career at WXYZ-AM, where he worked between 1973 and 1976. While there, he conducted what is believed to be the last interview with Jimmy Hoffa, the Teamster leader who disappeared July 30, 1975. Stanecki later sold the piece to *Playboy* magazine. The scoop brought Stanecki nationwide attention and a job at Channel 7. Although Stanecki's Newshawk persona made him one of the most recognized personalities in Detroit, it was no fun. "You'd be eating dinner someplace and somebody would sit down at your table and insist that you solve their problem right then and there," he recalls. Boozing was getting to be a problem. He later ended up on Channel 2 (1988-1990), where he turned in long-form pieces. As for the boozing, he got sober and wrote a book about the experience called *Life is a Joke, and God Wrote it*.

## Thomas, Ken (d: 1993)

A reporter/anchorman who worked at Channels 2, 7 and 50

Jerry Stanecki, the "Newshawk," helped viewers in need.

during the 1960s and 1970s. Thomas (real name: Kenneth Kitchin Jr.) started in Detroit broadcasting as a reporter at Channel 7. His coverage of Detroit's 1967 riot earned him awards and he was promoted to replace Bill Bonds on the Channel 7 anchor desk when Bonds left for Los Angeles in 1968.

But Thomas ran into the unstable side of the TV news business during the next half-dozen years. He worked for less than a year (1969-1970) at KABC-TV in Los Angeles before returning home to Detroit in early 1970 to anchor Channel 50's 10 p.m. newscast. However, Channel 50 cancelled the newscast within a year. Thomas worked briefly in Boston and Miami before returning again to Detroit in 1974—this time as an anchorman at Channel 2. But that, too, turned sour. Channel 2 officials had planned to pair Thomas with Jac Le Goff—a thought that made sense, since Thomas' lively style would probably have meshed well with Le Goff's more avuncular manner. But Le Goff jumped to Channel 7 before Thomas even arrived at Channel 2. Thomas' pairing with Woody Willis didn't work all that well. Thomas later said he never would have taken the Channel 2 job if he knew Le Goff wouldn't be on the premises. Joe Glover replaced Thomas in 1975. Thomas spent most of the rest of his life as a successful public relations man. At the time of his death in 1993, he was managing a radio station in Michigan's Upper Peninsula.

## Thompson, Anne

She became one of NBC News' busiest reporters after she left Channel 4 in the 1990s. A native of Boston, she joined Channel 4 as a street reporter. A near tragedy launched her into the top tier of Detroit street reporters. While covering street celebrations on Detroit's east side after the Detroit Pistons 1990 NBA championship, a mob surrounded her van and roughed her up. Thompson gamely went on the air immediately afterward to describe the experience.

Ken Thomas of Channels 2, 7 and 50.

During her years at Channel 4, she was often seen on the 11 p.m. newscast standing in front of a darkened building and explaining a tragedy that had happened hours before. After joining NBC News, her talents were put to better use. She was seen on *NBC Nightly News* most nights of the week covering national stories out of the Midwest. No more darkened buildings. No more car wrecks.

## Timmons, Robbie

Another survivor: more than 20 years at Channel 7, which she joined in 1982; and at Channel 2 for a half-dozen years before that. Timmons earned a B.A. from Ohio State University before becoming an anchor at Lansing's WILX-TV. She is married to Jim Brandstatter—which is of interest because Brandstatter played football for OSU's archrival, the University of Michigan. She's unflappable, anchoring with Bill Bonds for many years, and Frank Turner.

## Wade, Vince

Wade is the archetype of the tough investigative reporter, Detroit style. During his nearly quarter century in local TV news (Channel 7, 1972-1989; Channel 2, 1989-1996) he reported on significant drug busts, mob trials and political corruption.

A Texan by birth, Wade migrated across the Oklahoma border and worked his way through the University of Oklahoma as a radio news reporter. Upon graduation, he asked a pal in a local Associated Press bureau to recommend the top news stations in each market. Wade was told that WKNR-AM, then led by Phil Nye, was Detroit's news leader—despite WJR-AM's reputation. Wade impressed Nye, who put him on the WKNR payroll in 1969. When Nye took over leadership of Channel 7's newsroom in 1972, Wade followed.

Channel 7's news department was organized into a "beat" system during those days. Ven Marshall covered labor. Jim

Unflappable anchor Robbie Timmons.

143

Investigative reporter Vince Wade.

Herrington covered politics. Wade covered local corruption, developing significant sources at the local Federal Bureau of Investigation offices. More often than not, Wade could be seen reporting from U.S. District Court in Detroit, where the town's biggest public corruption cases were adjudicated. He covered the criminal case involving John Z. DeLorean, the ex-General Motors star who had been accused of bilking his firm's stockholders out of millions. (DeLorean was acquitted.)

By the time Wade abandoned the business in 1996, he was more often seen reporting from a freeway overpass, telling viewers what they already knew: That it was snowing outside. That frustrated Wade deeply, so he quit. "By the time I left, it was murder du jour, Kevorkian du jour, drive-by shooting du jour. I didn't see much effort to cover the news, as I defined it. People ask me if I miss it. My answer is that you can't miss what no longer exists."

## Weaver, Joe

In a business noted for instability, Weaver reported and anchored at Channel 2 for nearly 35 years. After breaking into the broadcast business as farm editor and baseball announcer for a Toledo radio station, Weaver came to Detroit in 1963 as an anchorman. He left the anchor desk in 1965, but continued as a street reporter and commentator until his retirement in 1993. Often, he covered the important labor and business stories of the day. His notes—nine boxes of them—can be found in Wayne State's Walter Reuther Library of Labor and Urban Affairs.

His own contribution to the wilder side of Detroit broadcasting history involved a 1969 scuffle between Weaver and the editor of *The South End,* Wayne State University's student newspaper. Weaver came to the newspaper to interview editor John Watson about a campus controversy. Watson offered only a string of "no comments" to Weaver's questions and shut an office door in

**The following is an excerpt from a program that aired 10:30 p.m. November 30, 1971. TV2 Reports: "What Do You Think?" Anchored by Joe Weaver, the station visited area malls in hopes of measuring public opinion. Here is what they found:**

"What is the most pressing problem facing our community? Ask a hundred people and you'll get a lot of different answers. We did just that over the past two months and surprisingly the majority of answers pinpointed six main subjects. As a matter of fact we visited four separate suburban shopping centers to sample public opinion. (They were Southland Center in Taylor; Northland in Southfield, Eastland in Harper Woods and Oakland Mall in Troy.)

"The six most pressing problems defined in our survey were:

Busing

Drug Abuse

Crime

Pollution

Race relations

And the Vietnam War."

*Source: Joe Weaver papers,*

*Walter P. Reuther Library of Labor and Urban Affairs*

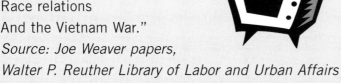

Weaver's face. A scuffle followed as cameras rolled. Weaver filed an assault charge against Watson. Replied Watson: "He was trespassing, abusive, provocative and disruptive to the operation of the office." A Recorder's Court jury acquitted Watson of assault charges. But the fight made for great television.

Channel 4's Dick Westerkamp: No. 1 in the 1950s and 1960s.

## Westerkamp, Dick

"Good evening, I'm Dick Westerkamp. The temperature in Detroit is _____."

News viewers of the 1950s and 1960s remember Westerkamp's opening mantra, and there were plenty of viewers who watched as he delivered the news—standing, from behind a podium. Westerkamp was Detroit's most-watched newscaster throughout most of the 1950s and 1960s. At one point, the Channel 4 team of Westerkamp, Sonny Eliot and Don Kremer more than doubled the ratings of the competition.

Westerkamp majored in journalism and art at the University of Cincinnati and Ohio State University, sticking with both endeavors throughout his life. After working in Ashland, Kentucky, and Buffalo, New York, he joined WWJ-TV in 1956, remaining there until 1968. Inside the Channel 4 newsroom, he was known for two things: his fastidious nature and the work he put into writing his nightly newscast. Later in TV news history, writers and producers would write scripts for the anchors. During the early days, the anchors did most of the writing. "He worked at it," recalls Ken Hissong, who worked at Channel 4 during the 1960s. "He'd check every fact."

His delivery was low-key and sober. "He had what I called the 'Ed Sullivan charm'," recalls Sonny Eliot, who worked alongside Westerkamp during Westerkamp's entire Detroit career. "He couldn't read a funny story to save his life and he'd screw up. People would see this and say, 'Heck, I can do better than that'—which is the same thing they said about Sullivan. But, as with Sullivan, they watched. Westerkamp had a sincerity that people believed in." Asked what attraction Westerkamp held for the Detroit audience, former Channel 4 News Director James Clark said: "I think it was his down-to-earth presentation. He'd come on many times and fluff his own name at the beginning. ... I think that people just learned to like the guy, because he had a straightforward way of presenting the news. ... I think sometimes they'd watch to see if he could get through a story all right." Westerkamp retired to Florida.

### Williams, Paul (d: 1983)

Paul Williams, Detroit's first anchorman.

Detroit's first full-time anchorman and original sportscaster could claim an awesome number of firsts: He anchored Detroit's first newscast in 1947 and called the first Tigers, Lions, Red Wings and University of Michigan football games—also in 1947.

An Oklahoma native, Williams first came to Detroit as a sportscaster. He was teamed up with Ty Tyson for University of Michigan football games and worked as a Detroit Tigers television broadcaster between 1947 and 1952. He was a Channel 4 newscaster between 1952 and 1962 and continued on as public affairs manager for another dozen years after he left the anchor desk. His perseverance was legendary. Williams once suffered a heart attack while reading the news, but stayed at his desk until the broadcast was finished.

# Sports

*At any given time, more Detroiters could probably name the nine starting Tigers than could name the nine members of the Detroit City Council. Detroit's interest in sports borders on obsession. These are the people who have helped satisfy that obsession.*

## Ackerman, Al

Throughout the 1960s and into the 1980s, he was Detroit's most controversial sportscaster. Before Ackerman hit town, sportscasters stuck with the scores. Ackerman introduced the idea of giving analysis and opinions, which he delivered in an acerbic, sometimes dyspeptic fashion. Ackerman questioned why Pontiac citizens—hard-working folks who mostly lived paycheck to paycheck—were being forced to build a stadium for William Clay Ford, one of the world's richest men. (He never referred to the Pontiac Silverdome as the "Silverdome." To him, it was the "Teflondome.") By the standards of today's sports talk radio, Ackerman seems like weak tea. Then, his work was cutting edge.

Ackerman learned television during the 1950s and 1960s at Grand Rapids' WOOD-TV, then considered one of the country's top local TV news operations. While Ackerman was in Grand Rapids, the station won a Peabody Award, broadcasting's highest

Outspoken sportscaster Al Ackerman coined the "Bless You Boys" phrase.

honor, for non-sports features on a weekly newsmagazine show called *Unit 8*. Ackerman was associated with the show. Later, he joined San Francisco's KCBS-AM as a sports-talk host, where he learned a valuable lesson: "I was midway between the University of California/Berkeley and Stanford University. So if you made a mistake, such as mispronouncing the name of a small town, you heard about it. What I learned there is that the audience is far more intelligent and perceptive than anybody in broadcasting gives them credit for."

Ackerman joined Channel 4 in 1964 and stayed until 1972. During those years, Ackerman and New York's Howard Cosell developed a novel way of looking at sportscasting. Ackerman thought sports deserved more than a guy reading a few scores, and tried to kick the craft up a few journalistic notches. This involved lacing the scores with analysis, opinions and real reporting.

A few seemingly innocuous comments about the 1972 Olympic Games got him fired from Channel 4. Two African-American athletes declined to stand at attention for the U.S. national anthem while receiving their medals, touching off much angry comment. Ackerman opined that the hubbub didn't amount to much, considering the fact that 11 young Israeli athletes had just been killed in Munich. Ackerman said as much, and was terminated. He was quickly hired at Channel 7, completing the Bonds-Kelly-Ackerman-Turner team that put Channel 7 in the ratings lead during the 1970s. He now remembers those years as the best of his life. "Essentially," he recalls, "they told me 'We like you just the way you are.'"

His stay at Channel 7 lasted for seven years, when he returned to Channel 4. The old management—the gang that had canned him in 1972—was long gone, replaced by a management team from Channel 4's new owners, Post-Newsweek. During the Detroit Tigers' 1984 championship season, Ackerman's "Bless You Boys" phrase became a popular saying. It was also the title of a season-recapping paperback and a local Top 10 recording that was on the charts for the entire summer of 1984. He even got to ride with the team during the 1984 ticker-tape parade in downtown Detroit. A botched leg operation that left Ackerman in constant pain ended his career in 1989, when he retired to Florida.

## Beat the Champ

Two Detroit cultural factors explain how *Beat the Champ* ran seven (yes, seven) nights a week on Channel 4, usually following the *Tonight* show. One is the popularity of bowling. During the 1960s, the era of the show's greatest popularity, some 250,000 locals bowled regularly. This made Detroit the "bowling capital of the world." The other factor was Detroit's unusual (at least compared to the rest of the country) habit of watching television past midnight. Most observers attribute the high late-night numbers to the high numbers of people who work odd shifts in factories. Whatever the case, *Beat the Champ* drew viewers by the thousands until Tom Snyder's national show knocked it off the air.

Created by Chuck Wahlbe, the show featured amateur bowlers locked in ten-pin combat for the right to take on a pro bowler. Prizes included, of course, color televisions.

## Bowling For Dollars

Channel 4's nightly bowling show, which aired between 1973 and 1979, mostly in the station's 7 p.m. weekday slot, made a television star out of radio's Bob Allison.

Bowlers vied for prizes ranging from a few bucks to an expensive Chevy Corvette, which went to the skilled (or lucky) bowler who threw five consecutive strikes. *Bowling For Dollars* was the classic Detroit show: It was shot at Allen Park's Thunderbowl Lanes—maybe the only show ever shot in the downriver area. The bowlers' families were introduced on the air, making neighborhood celebrities out of hundreds of otherwise regular folks.

**Mark Andrews (d: 2004), formerly WOMC-FM's sports director and also a Detroit native, rated his favorite sportscasters. Here is his list.**

### Pre-1975

Van Patrick, WJBK-TV2. He filled the time with a lot of information, and knew inside information on the Tigers and Lions, because he broadcast their games.

Don Wattrick, WXYZ-TV. He not only knew the four major sports but covered the others as well. He was the only Detroit sportscaster to become a general manager of a Detroit sports team, the Pistons.

Don Kremer, WWJ-TV. Called "Howdy Doody" by WWJ weatherman, Sonny Eliot, Kremer gave you all the information without the unnecessary glitz.

Honorable mention: Budd Lynch, WXYZ-TV, Bill Flemming, WJBK-TV.

### 1975-Present

Ray Lane, WJBK and WKBD-TV. For longevity alone, Lane gets this award. He was the most active sportscaster in the community, who cared not only for the big-time athletes, but the high school and amateur sports as well.

Al Ackerman, WWJ, WXYZ, WDIV. Changed the sportscasting business in Detroit. The team owners, some players and other sportscasters disliked him, but he was respected.

(Tie) Dave Diles, WXYZ-TV, and Don Shane WDIV-TV, WXYZ. Diles could have won the top award all by himself, but he came and went a few times to flirt with the network. He was too intelligent to be just a sportscaster.

Shane was outstanding when he was with WDIV, and came back as a strong anchor in 1990 at Channel 7.

Honorable mention: Charlie Neal, WJBK-TV, Anne Doyle WJBK-TV, Fred McLeod, WJBK, WDIV-TV.

The show started off slowly. But Allison, who'd hosted WWJ-AM's *Ask Your Neighbor* since 1962, was asked to fill in after the show had been on for about six weeks. Allison did something that would make a marketing person beam: He told *Ask Your Neighbor* listeners that the man behind the neighborly voice they'd been hearing on the radio could now be seen on TV. It worked. During most of its run, it drew top ratings in its time period. Nonetheless, Post-Newsweek killed the program after it bought the station during the late 1980s. Bowling, apparently, was not something that computed to the Post-Newsweek crowd.

The rights to the show were owned by Claster Productions, a Baltimore-based company that franchised the program to television stations across the country. But the Detroit ratings were usually larger than anywhere else in the country.

## Diles, Dave

Dave Diles, who was Channel 7's sportscaster from 1961-1972 and again between 1979-1982, was among the last local television broadcasters to train in the world of print journalism. Before being hired by Channel 7 in 1961, he had never been on television, except as a guest. Diles had just finished emceeing an event at the Redford's Western Golf and Country Club one evening when a man in sunglasses approached him. "I'd like to hire you," said the man. Replied Diles: "Why don't you call me in the event that you sober up?" The man in the sunglasses was Channel 7 General Manager John Pival. "Television was an accident," Diles recalled.

Diles grew up in Middleport, Ohio, some 100 miles south of Columbus. As a teenager, he contributed stories to the Gallipolis (Ohio) *Tribune*, Athens (Ohio) *Messenger*, and Pomroy (Ohio) *Sentinel*. He eventually worked his way into the Associated Press as a summer replacement reporter in Louisville, Kentucky, at a weekly salary of $52.50. He was eventually transferred to AP's Columbus bureau, where—on his first day on the job—he watched

Channel 7's Dave Diles.

a man die in the electric chair. Diles' lead: "Max Amerman went to death in Ohio's electric chair tonight with the Lord's Prayer on his lips." AP transferred Diles to Detroit in 1956, where Diles wrote sports and ran the wire service's regional sports coverage.

Pival initially tried to hire Diles as a late-night talk show host. Diles' friends, Sonny Eliot and Seymour Kapetansky, dissuaded him. "They asked: 'If you had a choice between watching Steve Allen, Jack Paar or you, who would you watch?'" Diles recalled. Instead, he settled for a job as a sportscaster, replacing Don Wattrick.

The transition went quite nicely. Not only did he appear on Channel 7's airwaves, he worked Saturdays as a sportscaster for ABC Sports. His first Channel 7 gig ended in 1972. He quit after Channel 7 hired Al Ackerman. However, Diles was hired back in 1979 to replace Ackerman, who returned to Channel 4. General Manager Jeanne Findlater's pitch: "The stage is set, the audience is waiting, the houselights have been dimmed and we need you to dance." So he did. "It was less fun," he recalled. Along the way, Diles has written eight books, including co-authorships of books with former Detroit Tigers pitcher Denny McLain and former Michigan State University coach Duffy Daugherty. Diles left TV, saying, "I wanted to get out before my boredom showed."

The Diles style was more journalistic, less hyper than the style popular at the beginning of the 21st century. He now lives in a rural area outside of Athens, Ohio.

## Doyle, Anne

Channel 2's Anne Doyle was in the vanguard of women sports reporters. Doyle, on the air between 1978 and 1983, opened the locker rooms to women journalists, earning plenty of discussion along the way.

Although Doyle is the daughter of longtime WWJ-AM sportscaster Vince Doyle (d: 1990), her pre-Channel 2 back-

Anne Doyle opened the locker room to women journalists.

ground was in news reporting. After graduation from the University of Michigan, she worked as a reporter and/or anchor in Lansing, Grand Rapids and Los Angeles before returning home to Detroit as a Channel 2 sports journalist. Time Inc. had successfully sued baseball Commissioner Bowie Kuhn to open the locker room to one of its female reporters—thus opening doors (literally) for women across the country. Within three weeks of the federal court ruling, Doyle was offered a job at Channel 2. "I remember my dad putting down his fork when I told him I'd been hired as a sports reporter," Doyle recalls. "His reaction about going into the locker room was, 'Absolutely, you have to go into the locker room. Otherwise, you won't have any credibility.'"

The reactions of others, however, were not as egalitarian. University of Michigan football coach Bo Schembechler and the late Tigers General Manager Jim Campbell, were not happy with the idea, says Doyle. As late as January 1979, the Tigers were telling Doyle she couldn't enter the locker room—thereby putting her at a competitive disadvantage with male reporters. (The day before Opening Day 1979, the Tigers reversed course.) "Personally, I'm opposed to it," Campbell told *Detroit News* columnist Joe Falls. "I believe our players have a right to their privacy. But this is the only way I can solve the problem … open the doors to everybody."

"There was a reaction of fear from sportswriters," Doyle continued. "Fear that the women would ruin it for everybody—that the teams would simply close the locker rooms to everyone."

That did not happen. Doyle eventually earned the trust of the players, and female sportswriters are no longer an oddity. "I worked hard to be a legitimate reporter," she said. "I was not just window dressing." *Free Press* columnist Charlie Vincent characterized her as "one of the most conscientious television sportscasters in our city."

One of her most famous on-air moments occurred when Detroit Lions Coach Monte Clark walked out of a group interview (with cameras rolling) because Doyle had asked about his seemingly dismal future—understandable because the Lions had just finished a 4-5 season, capping it off with a miserable 31-7 drubbing by the Washington Redskins.

She left Channel 2 in 1983 to become an independent corporate communications specialist. She worked for the Ford Motor Company, going on to become director of North America Communications, and now does freelance public relations.

## Flemming, Bill

Flemming was among the best-known hosts on ABC's *Wide World of Sports*, which debuted in 1961 and revolutionized sports journalism. But Flemming learned his craft at Channels 2 and 4 during the 1950s, working as a sportscaster and a voice on University of Michigan football games. And he lived in the Bloomfield Hills/Birmingham area all the while that he worked at *Wide World*, before leaving ABC Sports in 1986.

Flemming grew up in Ann Arbor and graduated from the University of Michigan in 1949. His initial career plans involved medicine. Instead, he fell into broadcasting at Ann Arbor's WUOM-AM, and later became the voice of U-M football in 1953 for Detroit's WWJ-AM.

His involvement with *Wide World* associated him with one of television's most revolutionary programs. The late Roone Arledge (d: 2001) fashioned new production techniques and changed TV forever. Jim McKay, Flemming's co-host, became a star. And Flemming got to fly off to all kinds of neat places—Hawaii to cover surfing events, or Augusta, Georgia, to cover The Masters golf tournament. Often, he got there by flying his own plane out of Detroit.

Former *Detroit News* staff writer Lowell Cauffiel once asked Flemming why he stayed in Detroit. The answer: "I never liked

New York and always thought I'd just end up back here anyway. Then I got to thinking, what good is it to have two announcers who are the mainstays of *Wide World of Sports* in the same place? If the airports got fogged in, nobody is available. I convinced Roone Arledge that it was the right thing to do."

After leaving ABC, Flemming did freelance sports work before retiring in 1995.

## Harwell, Ernie

First, a salute from Al Kaline: "Ernie Harwell is the epitome of what a professional announcer should be," Kaline wrote in the introduction to Harwell's autobiography, *My 60 Years In Baseball*. Although primarily known as the radio voice of the Detroit Tigers, Harwell spent plenty of time in the television booth, as well: He served as the team's television announcer between 1960-1964—the first three of those years with George Kell, the last of those years with former Tigers Manager Bob Scheffing. Harwell also worked as the Tigers cable television voice (1993-1997) and went back again to television on Channel 50 in 1997.

Harwell's career was already well established before he got to Detroit in 1960. He had announced for the Brooklyn Dodgers (1948-1949), New York Giants (1950-1953) and Baltimore Orioles (1954-1959). He was NBC-TV's national television announcer for Bobby Thomson's home run to win the 1951 pennant over Brooklyn. No kinescope exists. However, it is said to be one of the most famous games in the history of sports. It was Kell who recommended Harwell to Stroh Brewery Co. President John Stroh—the Tigers club's biggest sponsor. So Harwell got the job, which he performed for the next decades with single-minded honesty and class.

## Heilmann, Harry (d: 1951)

Baseball fans still see his name posted in the center field stands

Ernie Harwell, "Long gone..."

at Comerica Park. Harry Heilmann was the first Hall of Fame player to work the Tigers television booth, sharing broadcast duties with Ty Tyson (d: 1968) and Van Patrick (d: 1974) during Detroit TV's first four years, 1947-1951.

Heilmann's career highlights included batting titles in 1921, 1923, 1925 and 1927. In one of those years, 1923, he hit .403. "People nowadays just don't realize how great a hitter Harry was," Ty Cobb remarked in an assessment that can be found on baseball-reference.com. "Next to Hornsby, he was the best right-handed hitter of them all." Heilmann's baseball career stretched from 1914 until 1932, with all but two of those years in a Tiger uniform.

However, Heilmann was to go on to a second career after retiring as a player. He joined WXYZ as a Tiger announcer in 1934, where he worked until 1950. (Between 1927 and 1942, Tigers games could also be heard on WWJ, with Ty Tyson calling the action.) When Detroit television got its start in 1947, Heilmann, Tyson and Paul Williams shared broadcast duties.

Heilmann died the day before the 1951 All-Star game, and was inducted into baseball's Hall of Fame the same year.

## Hockey Night In Canada

*Hockey Night In Canada* is not a local program. But it should have been, given that the program was ritual viewing for Detroit Baby Boomers. Detroit's television stations, when they carried the Wings at all, often joined the game in progress. By default, *Hockey Night In Canada* became the most consistent, most knowledgeable television source for area hockey fans. With only six teams in the National Hockey League, the Detroit Red Wings had a reasonable chance of appearing on the telecast.

Foster Hewitt's classic introduction, "Hello Canada and hockey fans in the United States and Newfoundland," became one of the best-known phrases in sports broadcasting. The program is still strong, although its importance to Red Wing fans has dimmed.

*Hockey Night In Canada* began as a radio broadcast. A bit of trivia: HNIC's first coast-to-coast broadcast was a 1933 battle between the Red Wings and Toronto Maple Leafs. The show began on television in 1952.

## Jamison, Red (d: 1979)

He was on Detroit television for only 18 months during the mid-1970s, and he worked mostly on weekends, but Red Jamison was one of the most talked about on-air personalities of that era. Jamison simply didn't look or sound like anybody else from here. His good-old-boy accent, leisure suits and goofy smile set him apart from slicker sportscasters who worked the airwaves at the time. Unfortunately, they also made him the butt of jokes around town.

Daniel Joseph Jamison's broadcasting experience before his 1975 arrival in Detroit included work at a Virginia radio station and as a sports director in Huntsville, Alabama. Channel 2 executives had in mind somebody different to handle sports and hired Jamison. They got their wish. Jamison was certainly different. But within a year, the station's consultants privately told station management that viewers weren't taking to Jamison. They dumped Jamison and replaced him with Charlie Neal, a black sportscaster who had been working at WJR-AM. Jamison later filed suit for wrongful dismissal, alleging that he had been dumped because he was white.

After Jamison's death, a jury awarded his estate $235,000, but a judge set the award aside because she felt that Jamison's lawyer hadn't established a connection between his death and the firing.

The few remaining years of Jamison's life after leaving Channel 2 were difficult. He worked in Scranton, Pennsylvania, and Columbus, Ohio, before returning to Nashville. He had trouble getting work in television, so he took a night job as a clerk.

He committed suicide by hanging, July 25, 1979.

Read the roll of those that played
Count every face; the crowds that made
A church of light; a field of dreams
A century of us; our team

Farewell the sun, and bar the gates
As fades the final roar
The brightest home; our eager youth
Like summer is no more

But ah, the blue and green of it
The light upon the field
The noise, the smell, the crowd, the sky
A common heart revealed

The many, one; in summer's sun
We pulled the runners home
A grassy sea, an English "D"
The athletes' skill a poem

The memories stray in twilight's fade
Was Boone at first...or third?
Did Kaline stem the Cardinal tide?
Who was it caught The Bird?

*Continued on pg. 161*

## Kaline, Al

Neither sports nor broadcasting is known for stability. But consider Detroit Tiger player/broadcaster Al Kaline's steady track record: Twenty-two seasons as a Tiger player (1953-1974) and another 26 seasons as the franchise's television broadcaster (1976-2001). Few players in the history of Major League Baseball stuck with a team on the field for two decades—less than 20, according to expert estimates. Stan Musial played with the St. Louis Cardinals for as many years. Baltimore Oriole Brooks Robinson and Boston Red Sox star Carl Yastrzemski are probably the only players of Kaline's caliber who stayed with one franchise longer. The combined tenure of 48 years made Kaline a living symbol of the franchise's greatness, which is particularly valuable in years when the franchise wasn't that great. He also displayed manners from another era, referring to John Fetzer or Mike Ilitch as Mr. Fetzer or Mr. Ilitch.

Although not a natural broadcaster, Kaline showed the same integrity and attention to detail in the booth that he showed on the field. When a Tiger player screwed up, Kaline never hid the truth. This earned Kaline credibility, the most invaluable capital a broadcaster can have. "Kaline the broadcaster was never the equal of Kaline the player. That would be hard for him, or any broadcaster," remarked *New York Times* sports writer Joe Lapointe, a native Detroiter. "But behind the microphone, he was honest and comprehensive. He was demanding about fundamentals and nuances of the game. For instance: If a player in the on-deck circle was watching a teammate running toward home plate for a slide, Kaline would notice whether or not that on-deck man moved the discarded bat out of the way. If he didn't, Kaline would let you know."

## Kell, George

His soft, soothing Arkansas twang brought the Detroit Tigers to television audiences between 1959 and 1996. The sound of Kell's voice, along with Ernie Harwell's, was the true signal that summer had arrived.

Kell, a native of Swifton, Arkansas, had a good career as a baseball player. His Major League career lasted between 1943 and 1956, including years with the Tigers at third base between 1946 and 1952. He first broke into broadcasting on CBS-TV, where he worked for $15,000 a year doing weekend baseball telecasts until Detroit Tigers owner John Fetzer talked Kell into returning to Detroit as a Tigers broadcaster for $20,000 annually. At the time, the Tigers needed a replacement for Mel Ott, who had died in an automobile accident.

Fetzer, who made a fortune in broadcasting before buying the Tigers, gave Kell some advice. Kell recounted Fetzer's counsel: "Don't try to be something you are not because it will never work. The fans will see through that immediately. I hired you because you are George Kell and because you have a gift for calling a game. Now just go out and be George Kell."

And that's what George Kell did. At first, he handled the middle three innings during the 1959 season with Van Patrick. The next year, Kell teamed with Ernie Harwell. The two handled games for both radio and TV audiences until the end of the 1963 season, when Kell quit to spend more time with his family in Arkansas. Fetzer, who didn't want to lose Kell, gave Kell the 1964 season off with half pay until the two could work out an arrangement that would allow Kell to spend more time at home. The arrangement eventually worked out by Fetzer: Ernie Harwell would handle all radio games, while Kell would work 45 games a year on television. The arrangement held until Kell retired after the 1996 season. His career spanned two stations (Channels 2 and 4), a string of managers, two World Series championships and one offer to manage the team—which he declined after the 1966 season. Had Kell taken the job, he could have been in the dugout for the 1968 championship season. Kell said he never second-guessed his refusal.

*Continued from pg. 160*

But recalled exactly in our hearts
We loved our time; this place
100 years; let's go!...play ball!
The thrill, this park, its grace

Echoes carry; springtimes fly
Now autumns' shadows' yield
Forever winter drapes the cry
"Long gone" across the field

If there be ghosts that know the land;
Called back to hallowed scenes
My father and my father's dad
Still hold this field of dreams

That section there, in leftfield high
My father and I came
And then, in turn, I brought my son
To our eternal game

So read the roll of those that played
Count every face; the crowds that made
A church of light; a field of dreams
A century of us...the team

Above all, Kell was a gentleman in the booth. The only slip that even bordered on questionable taste was when a crazed fan ran onto the field and got into a shoving match with Tiger right fielder Kirk Gibson. Even after three or four shoves, the security guards still hadn't arrived to haul the rogue fan away, causing Kell to say: "For chrissakes … is nobody gonna help Gibson?" Kell, a regular attendee of services at Swifton United Methodist Church, was probably more mortified by his own remark than anybody else. "That's the only thing I can ever remember saying on the air that I wish my mind could have slowed down my tongue," he later wrote in his autobiography, *Hello Everybody, I'm George Kell.* Off season, Kell's world went far beyond baseball. He owned a successful Arkansas car dealership, kept about 1,100 acres of Arkansas farmland, involved himself in Arkansas politics (helping Dale Bumpers get elected to the Arkansas governor's chair before Bill Clinton got there), and served on the Arkansas Highway Commission.

This is the way Kell summed almost four decades behind the microphone: "All I ever tried to do with my broadcasts was to tell the story about the game going on out on the field. I tried to tell it with the honesty and decency that was bred into me ever since I was a boy and with the insight of somebody who happened to be very lucky in the game."

## Klitenic, Stu

Klitenic worked as sports anchor/reporter for Channels 2 and 7 and handled color commentary on Detroit Pistons radio broadcasts, all between 1983 and 1989. Most fans remember his hands, which were perpetual motion machines.

Klitenic entered journalism via the basketball court. A standout high school athlete, the 6-foot 5-inch Klitenic attended the University of South Carolina on a basketball scholarship. When he realized that he'd never make the pros, Klitenic began looking for something else. His search ended in the University of South Carolina journalism department, which was located in the same building as the university's athletic department. "I fell in love with journalism," he says. "It was a perfect fit." He earned both bachelor's and master's degrees in journalism.

Klitenic arrived in Detroit in 1983 following stops in Richmond, Virginia, and Columbus, Ohio—each a year and a half. Following his Detroit stint, he worked in St. Louis, Missouri, and Atlanta, Georgia, where he currently resides. Currently, Klitenic can be seen anchoring sports for CNN Headline News.

## Kremer, Don

Don Kremer's resume: He not only was the Channel 4's sports maven between 1960 and 1976, he also served as the radio voice of University of Michigan football, host of the *Beat the Champ* bowling program, which aired seven nights a week, play-by-play man for the now-defunct Detroit Wheels football team, and a sportscaster for WWJ-AM.

A graduate of Michigan State University, Kremer first signed on at Channel 2, where he subbed for Bill Flemming. Kremer later skipped to Channel 4, where he became one of Detroit's most respected sports broadcasters. U-M football fans liked the way he handled Wolverine football, mostly because he wasn't Bob Ufer. Weatherman Sonny Eliot liked Kremer because Eliot could call him "Howdy Doody" on the air. Bowling fans liked him because he hosted *Beat the Champ* every night after *The Tonight Show with Johnny Carson*. In fact, a week of *Champ* was taped in one long day of taping. "By the end of the day," he joked, "I got so sick of balls rolling up and down the lanes I could scream."

Kremer could have had a longer career, but quit suddenly in late 1976, when he slipped a letter beneath the general manager's door and walked out of the station for good. "I just got sick of the

Channel 4's Don Kremer.

business," he recalled later. "I was especially unhappy with the way they were treating some of the employees. I felt we were a family, but they weren't treating some of the employees that way." His bosses were shocked at his resignation, with one of his supervisors telling reporters that he was "stunned" by the resignation and tried to get Kremer to reconsider. Kremer went on to become public relations director for the Detroit Lions for eight years before retiring permanently from sports in the mid-1980s.

## Lane, Ray

Since beginning his career at Channel 2 in 1961, Lane has worked as WJBK-TV's sports anchor (1961-1982); announced Detroit Tigers games on WJR-AM (1965-1973); and anchored Channel 50's sportscasts (1985-1996). As of this writing, he continues on Channel 50 as an interviewer during Detroit Red Wings hockey games. And, most notable of all, he is still refreshingly "shtickless." Sports announcers, it seems, have to have a shtick—whether it be Van Earl Wright's booming "DEEP" to Bernie Smilovitz's bloopers. All Lane ever did was report sports in a credible, journalistic manner. What a concept!

A Detroit native (Mackenzie High School, Michigan State University), Lane briefly contemplated life as a major league baseball player before washing out of the Chicago White Sox system. While his baseball career was stillborn, his life in TV and radio was just beginning. He worked in Waterloo, Iowa, and Bay City, Cadillac and Flint, Michigan, before joining Channel 2 in 1961.

In a career filled with accomplishments, his most important was his work with the Detroit Tigers between 1965 and 1973. That included the championship 1968 season, an indelible memory for every Detroit Baby Boomer. It seemed like Lane would go on forever, but he was fired in 1982 by Channel 2 General Manager Bill Flynn, although there was no shame in that: Flynn became nationally famous for firing just about everybody at Channel 2, includ-

Ray Lane, Channels 2 and 50.

ing Joe Glover and Sonny Eliot. Lane did everything during the next three years—Cincinnati Reds baseball, college football and basketball. Finally, Channel 50 hired him in 1985, where he continued on in his straightforward, informative fashion.

## Lynch, Budd

Lynch is known best as the television voice of hockey's Detroit Red Wings, which he was between 1949-75. But the body of Lynch's broadcasting work is wider and broader than a hockey rink. He appeared on Channels 2, 4, 7 and 9 doing wrestling, college football, baseball highlights, boxing, billiards, horseracing and bowling. Although retired from broadcasting, his sporty baritone has been heard over the public address system at Wings games at Joe Louis Arena since 1985.

Lynch, who grew up in Windsor and elsewhere, served in the Canadian Army during World War II as a member of the Essex Scottish Infantry. An 88-millimeter shell tore off Lynch's right arm during a 1944 battle in France. While recuperating, he began working for the British Broadcasting Corporation, producing *Combat Diary*, which aired 4 p.m. daily. Upon returning from Europe, he did play-by-play for the Windsor Spitfires. Ty Tyson, a veteran Detroit broadcaster, talked Lynch into producing a show on Channel 4, but Red Wings owner Jack Adams suggested Lynch get an on-air tryout. "My tryout lasted 25 years," he recalled.

Curiously, few people detected Lynch's war injury. "On TV, people didn't notice I had an empty sleeve," he said. "Then I'd go to a banquet or a Boy Scout meeting and people would ask: 'What happened?'"

Lynch is fond of saying, "You measure a man by what he has, not what he doesn't have." What he also had was credibility. "Here is a guy who rode the train with Gordie Howe and Sid Abel," said producer Toby Cunningham. "All of that background served the viewers well." Budd's collection of "one-arm" jokes is legendary.

Budd Lynch, voice of the Detroit Red Wings.

"I must have been about 19 or 20 and was thinking I'd like to be a sportscaster. So several people suggested I call Ray. At the time, he was the No. 1 guy at Channel 2. As I recall, the appointment was for 2:30 p.m. I probably showed up something like four hours early and just waited in the lobby.

"He took me aside for at least half an hour, and we talked about all kinds of things: What I wanted to do, things I liked about Detroit sports and sportscasters. It was like he was my best friend. Whenever I called after that, he always returned my call. If he couldn't talk to me immediately, he'd ask: 'Can I call you back?' He'd call back about five minutes later, then apologize for not being able to talk to me immediately. Ray was a huge inspiration to me. Later, after I found my first job as a sportscaster in the Upper Peninsula, I'd call him for advice. And he'd yell at me for not calling collect. He'd yell 'You're not making any money. You're making $1.60 an hour.

"For years, I thought maybe I was getting some sort of special treatment. He and my father were fraternity brothers, or something. I thought maybe that was it. But after I got a job at Channel 50 I found out that he provided the same sort of guidance to anybody who asked. Anybody. He'd get calls from students at University of Detroit Mercy, Wayne State, Specs Howard, University of Michigan, wherever, and he'd take the time to help. He'd take them to ball games, talk about broadcasting—anything they wanted.

"To this day, I get angry anytime I hear anybody criticize Ray Lane. Somebody complains, 'Gee, he's really old' and I go nuts. Because he really helped me at a time when I could use all of the help I could get. I remember calling him once. I told him, 'You've done all of this for me, but I've done nothing for you.' I asked him, 'What do I owe you? Because I really owe you.' And you know what he said? 'Pass it on. Pass on this kind of help to the next group.'"

## Martyn, Bruce

Martyn's 31-year career as a Red Wings broadcaster is among the longest in modern Detroit sports broadcasting. The first two-thirds of his career, which lasted from 1964 until 1995, involved television. For the record, it was Martyn's voice that marshaled Channel 50's on-air debut.

Martyn broke into radio in his native Sault Ste. Marie, where he did everything from high school sports to news at WSOO-AM. He moved to Detroit in 1953 when he landed at WCAR-AM. "I did Michigan State University football on Saturdays, Detroit Lions football on Sundays," recalled Martyn. The Stroh Brewery Co., a Red Wings sponsor, offered Martyn a job in 1964. He has been honored with the National Hockey League's Foster Hewitt Award.

## Ott, Mel (d: 1958)

Ott was the second in a string of Hall of Fame players to sit in the Detroit Tigers TV booth, the first being Harry Heilmann. His hiring was unusual because Ott had no Detroit connection before joining the Tigers organization as a broadcaster in 1956. (Other athletes, such as Dizzy Trout and Harry Heilmann, had played with the team.) Nevertheless, he became quite popular.

Baseball historians consistently rank Ott among the very top level of players such as Babe Ruth, Lou Gehrig and Jimmie Fox. Ott's numbers were stunning: 511 home runs and a lifetime .304 batting average. Those numbers made him a hero in New York, where he played between 1926 and 1947—all with the New York Giants. He left baseball in 1953, but rejoined the sports world in 1956 as Van Patrick's broadcast partner in Detroit.

Less manic or unpredictable than his predecessor, Dizzy Trout, Ott worked out well. "He may not have been as smooth as others," recalls Ernie Harwell, "but he was extremely likable. Everybody liked Mel Ott." George Kell replaced Ott after Ott's death following an off-season automobile crash in Mississippi in 1958.

## Parker, John

Parker (real name: John Freshwater) anchored sports at Channel 4 throughout the 1950s. He was most famous around Channel 4 for a verbal brawl with Doc Greene (d: 1970), the famed *Detroit News* columnist who had published a collection of columns entitled *Dies a Crapshooter*. Parker, interviewing Greene, referred to the book as "Dies a Grasshopper." Greene didn't think this was funny, and the two went at it. Both Parker and Greene had reputations as serious drinkers, leading most contemporary observers to surmise that both were in their cups. Parker was eventually fired in 1960 for a drunken on-air incident, and was replaced by Don Kremer.

## Patrick, Van (d: 1974)

Patrick's nickname, "the ole announcer," has a relaxed feel to it. But Patrick, considered Detroit's premier sportscaster throughout the 1950s, 1960s and 1970s, held as many as four jobs simultaneously. At one time during the 1960s and 1970s, he handled sportscasting chores for Channel 2, play-by-play duties for both Notre Dame University football and the Detroit Lions, and served as sports director for the Mutual Broadcasting System.

Patrick's portly, 250-pound physique never betrayed it, but he was a star college athlete in his native Texas. He played football at Texas Christian University, but made it big on radio when he went live for 13 consecutive hours describing a fire in a small Texas town in 1937. "NBC picked up a half-hour of my description and from that time on, my career was pretty well set," he once said. Patrick moved into big-time sports in 1946 when he was hired as play-by-play man for the Cleveland Indians. Within two years, he broadcast the first World Series ever telecast on TV and was then hired on WJR-AM as sports director in 1949.

That turned out to be the beginning of maybe the most successful career in the history of local electronic sports journalism.

"The ole announcer," Van Patrick.

Patrick started broadcasting for the Tigers on radio as an assistant to Harry Heilmann, who died later that year. Patrick got the No. 1 slot in 1952, working with legends Dizzy Trout and Mel Ott. Patrick was fired from the Tigers job in 1959 after eight seasons because he had been associated with the wrong beer. The Stroh Brewing Co. bought the sponsorship of the Tigers games. Unfortunately for Patrick, he was connected with the previous sponsor—the Goebel Brewing Co. Was he bitter? Maybe. Shortly after being fired, he told an audience at a downtown Detroit party: "It hasn't been easy trying to make those Tigers look good. Now let somebody else lie about them for a while."

His work habits were prodigious: He was Channel 2's top sportscaster between 1960 and 1974; and did the Lions on both radio and television between 1950 and 1967, when he was forced to choose between radio and television (he chose radio).

All of these gigs made him rich. At the time of his death, he was pulling in $100,000 annually. And he was part-owner of WKNR. Patrick talked to *Detroit News* staff writer Al Stark only weeks before his death in 1974: "When I think back, I wonder why I felt I had to work seven days a week all those years."

He had the words "ole announcer" printed on the cuffs of his shirts.

## Redmond, Mickey

As of this writing, Redmond has been the Detroit Red Wings television commentator for some 16 years. Redmond's unique way of expressing himself promoted a group of fans to start a Mickey Redmond Quote Page on the Internet. A few examples: "He was born at night, but not this night."… "A hockey player without a stick is like a duck without wings."… "Toronto's just hanging around there like a bad smell right now." … "The (Anaheim Mighty) Ducks look like they're skating in sand."

Redmond broke into hockey as a teenager, joining the

Peterborough Petes in 1963. His 10-year National Hockey League career included four seasons with the Montreal Canadiens and six with the Wings. Highlights included back-to-back 50-plus goal seasons with the Wings, when Redmond popped 52 and 51 goals respectively in 1972-73 and 1973-74.

There is no shortage of retired hockey players roaming about, but few with Redmond's distinctive way of calling a game. The best sportscasters have their trademark expressions. Here are a few more of Mickey's, courtesy of the Mickey Redmond Quote Page: "Ei-yi-yi" … "Holy Mackerel" … "Bingo, bango."

## Smilovitz, Bernie

Channel 4's Bernie Smilovitz is the most influential Detroit sportscaster of the 1980s and 1990s. As cable's ESPN and sports talk radio became more important for rabid sports fans, TV stations looked increasingly to sportscasters who would appeal to non-sports fans. The idea: Keep folks who cared not a whit for sports from tuning out. Smilovitz, with his hambone clowning and "Let's go to the tape" shtick did that as well as anybody in Detroit TV. Of course, people who were into sports felt that Smilovitz trivialized their world.

A native of Washington, D.C., Smilovitz worked in his native city before signing on at Channel 4 as Eli Zaret's replacement in 1986. He was so successful that he ended up at WCBS-TV, the CBS-owned station in New York. That turned out to be a disaster for Smilovitz—and no fun. The newspaper columnists took turns teeing off on Smilovitz. Soon, the station's entire front line— three anchors, three reporters and sportscaster Smilovitz—were fired simultaneously one evening. Only the weather guy avoided the flying shrapnel. Smilovitz returned home to Channel 4.

## Trout, Dizzy (d: 1972)

This raconteur, a 1940s-era Detroit Tigers pitching star, brought his anecdotal style to the Tigers broadcast booth between 1953 and 1955. Describing Trout's approach to color commentary, *New York Times* columnist Arthur Daley called Trout the team's "built-in loudspeaker," "the most colorful and talkative person in the Detroit entourage" and "a wholesome, disrupting force."

Trout pitched for the team between 1939 and 1952, reaching his zenith on the mound during the 1944 and 1945 seasons. He won 27 games for the Tigers in 1944, posting the lowest earned-run average in Major League Baseball and bringing the team to the brink of the American League pennant. (The St. Louis Browns won it on the last day of the season.) Trout returned the next year to win 18 games, burnishing the legend with a stunning display of stamina during the final weeks of the 1945 season: He pitched six games in nine days, winning four. The Tigers took the World Series that year.

Trout's conversational dexterity and stamina made him a star in the broadcast booth, too. Teamed with Van Patrick, Trout referred to himself as "Ol' Diz" and spun one baseball story after another. A sample (again, from a 1955 Arthur Daley column): "There was a time in Washington when the temperature was 105 degrees. It was so hot my glasses kept fogging up on me. So I went to bat against Allan Gettel without my glasses. Couldn't see a thing. So I hit a home run. As I ran around the bases Gettel never stopped calling me 'a blind slob.'"

Trout took one more spin on the mound, in 1957 with the Baltimore Orioles. He joined the Chicago White Sox club as a pitching instructor, later becoming a public relations man with the team.

## Tyson, Ty (d: 1968)

One of Tyson's eulogists wrote that Tyson "was to several generations of Michigan sports fans the last word—and for years the only word—in local sportscasting." Tyson (given name: Edwin Lloyd Tyson) handled Detroit Tigers radio broadcasts between

Dizzy Trout was a "wholesome, disrupting force" in the Tigers broadcast booth.

Ty Tyson, Detroit's first sportscaster.

1927 and 1942. When television came along, Tyson served as WWJ-TV's baseball commentator until the early 1950s.

A native of Pennsylvania and a World War I veteran, he was hired at WWJ in 1922. Tyson chalked up a number of firsts: He worked the first Tigers radio broadcast on April 19, 1927; and the first University of Michigan football game, in 1924. Detroiters heard about the opening of the Ambassador Bridge and the Detroit-Windsor tunnel from Tyson, who anchored the radio specials celebrating the debuts. Tyson worked as a television commentator for Tigers baseball between 1947 and 1952.

One can accurately say that Tyson lived and died with baseball. The physician attending Tyson at the time of the broadcaster's death remarked that "we talked about baseball and the World Series" until Tyson went into a coma. He was 80 when he died.

## Wattrick, Don (d: 1965)

Wattrick, a pioneer sportscaster, participated in the sports he covered—and at both ends of his broadcasting career. A graduate of Central Michigan University, he earned a football letter 1931, and later played basketball for the Alpena Independents and the Hamtramck Belmont Trenchers. With his athletic career finished, he went into broadcasting, handling sports chores at both WXYZ radio and television from 1942 to 1962. He was so popular, Soupy Sales created a spoof character by the name of "Juan Dottrick." Wattrick was replaced by Dave Diles in 1962.

Although his broadcasting career had taken a hit by the early 1960s, his career in sports was not over. He was tapped as general manager of the Detroit Pistons in 1964. (To grasp such a move, imagine Bernie Smilovitz as general manager of the Pistons.) Wattrick's first move was to appoint Dave DeBusschere as player/coach. DeBusschere (d: 2003), 24 at the time, is still the youngest National Basketball Association coach ever. Wattrick died of a heart attack within a year of taking the Pistons job. He was 55.

Channel 7's Don Wattrick.

# Zaret, Eli

He was one of the pre-eminent sportscasters of the 1980s, and one of the last local sportscasters who emphasized journalism over show-biz elements. Howard Cosell, one of Zaret's heroes, popularized the concept that sports and journalism were not mutually exclusive. Later, Al Ackerman carried it further, and Zaret even further still. But soon, fashions in local television changed. Comedians who adhered to the concept that standup comedy and sports should be intertwined became more of the rage.

A native of Nutley, New Jersey, Zaret graduated from the University of Michigan in 1972 and learned the craft of broadcasting at a series of radio stations—WJZZ-FM, WABX-FM, and WRIF-FM. Channel 4 gave Zaret a shot at the TV medium, and he did well. When the Detroit Tigers made their now-famous run for the World Series in 1984, Zaret did the Tigers pre-game show. It made him almost as famous as many of the Tigers themselves. Then, New York came calling. A New York sports gig is the dream of most sports broadcasters, and he made a go of it at WABC-TV. The *New York Times* introduced Zaret to the New York television audience as a broadcaster "who brings to the job a deep, raspy voice and a prior reputation as an anti-establishment radio commentator at several Detroit rock music stations."

But Zaret soon discovered what many discover, to their sorrow: New York local television is not necessarily a fun place. Zaret lasted less than a year at WABC, returning to Detroit as Channel 2's top sportscaster. But the impact wasn't quite the same. Channel 2 didn't carry the Tigers. And television had changed. Cable television soaked up the hard-core sports audience during the 1980s and 1990s.

More recently, he was heard on WXYT-AM sports talk radio's "The Locker Room." The show was canceled in January 2004. He recently wrote a book, *The Last of the Great Tigers*, about the team's 1984 championship season.

# Weather

*Television weathercasting is an unusual mix of physics and show biz. Some among this group were pure science. Others were a little song, a little dance and a little seltzer down your pants. Whatever their style, they told us what was about to fall from the sky.*

## Eliot, Sonny

Sonny Eliot is the consummate example of Detroit TV's uniqueness. Part comic, part vaudeville entertainer, part serious student of the craft and technique of entertainment, it is safe to say there has never been anybody like him in the country. Anytime. Anywhere.

Eliot (real name: Marvin Schlossberg) was born at Hastings and Farnsworth. His parents, Jenny and Jacob, ran a hardware store. Eliot ended up spending hours in the Warfield Theater. "It was my baby-sitter," he later recalled. Eliot's older brother worked as a drummer in a big band, and allowed Eliot to watch rehearsals. By then, he was hooked on entertainment. He was amused, amazed and captivated by what made people laugh.

Eliot refined his curiosity at Wayne State University, where he studied under Fran Stryker, the producer/writer of The *Lone Ranger*. While still in college, Eliot heard one of his *Lone Ranger* scripts put on the air.

Sonny Eliot: Fog + Drizzle = "Fozzle."

Eliot and his wife, the lovely Annette, at the Thanksgiving Day Parade, circa 1964.

**Although he began his career as a straight weatherman, Sonny Eliot quickly morphed into something of a comic—the kind of guy who'd work jokes into his weathercast every few minutes. He describes the transition.**

"I'd been doing it (the weather) for several months very straight, very meteorologically—giving lapse rates, temperatures, prognosis charts and doing all of the things you're supposed to do to make it a serious presentation. It became kind of mundane.

"One day, I saw I had a temperature in Las Vegas, and it was 55 degrees there—very chilly. I said, 'Five and five—10 the hard way.' Paul Williams, who was doing the news, started to smile. I said to myself: 'Hey that's pretty good. I got a smile from Williams.' Next thing, I gave the temperature in Florida—'It's 82 degrees in Florida, where businessmen lie on the beach—about how much money they make.' That was the development of it, those two in the same newscast. Then I started tinkering with it, finding out that there were certain things you could do.

"It was like when you went to college: The instructor tried to sweeten the course, gave you the information but made it interesting, or humorous. That's the way it developed. It didn't develop overnight. Giving the temperature in a foreign city in the language of that city—that just happened. I knew German. Then I did it in French. I can do it in 15, 16 languages—only the numbers, of course.

"One day I got caught on saying the word Engadine. I got stuck on it—Enga, Enga, Enga. If you're in hot water, you might as well take a bath. So as long as I fluffed it, I kept on fluffing it. And that caught on, too."

During the 1940s, he also had a bit part in the biggest drama of the 20th century: World War II. Shot down over Germany, he became an unwelcome guest of the Nazis as a prisoner of war. One night, on a bombing run, his plane began going down. Eliot managed to unleash his bombs before hitting the earth, but was captured by what Eliot later described as "the village idiot" and turned over to the authorities. Eliot still has a collection of his prisoner of war artifacts. Kept in a bound leather book, the collection includes a small envelope containing a bit of coffee from the camp, a swatch from his blanket and the card the Nazis kept on Eliot.

Some of the technology of World War II helped make TV possible, and that's where Eliot wanted to be. During the early days of television, versatility was the key. Nobody had ever imagined a medium like that, so nobody knew what he or she was doing. "Whenever somebody asked something, I'd say yes," he said. When Channel 4 producers dreamed up a puppet show in 1948 called *Willy Dooit* they wanted to know if Eliot could do accents. Yes, he could do that. When the producers thought up a golf show in which an amateur took lessons from a golf pro, they asked Eliot if he could golf. Eliot said yes to that, too. So when Channel 4 decided it needed somebody to do the weather, Eliot was asked about that, too. By then, on paper, Eliot would have been perfectly qualified for the job. Eliot was one of the few people with actual television experience. As a pilot during World War II, he knew something about weather. The job was his from 1949 to 1981. (Later, he did weather at Channel 2 between 1981-1982.)

As the weatherman, Eliot did two things: Of course, he served up weather—to viewers, one of a TV station's most important services. And he also injected broad levity to the evening newscast. Ven Marshall, Dick Westerkamp, Britton Temby and Bill Fyffe were serious guys—and being serious is a fine trait for a journalist. But Eliot livened the place up, so the news didn't look like *Apocalypse Now*.

Eliot became the station's "go to" guy, the on-air personality Channel 4 used in numerous ways. During the early 1950s, the station created a game show called *Hit A Homer*, in which contestants advanced a base or two after answering questions of varying degrees of difficulty. (The harder the question, the more bases a contestant got.) Eliot hosted that program. Channel 4 came up with *Shadow Stumpers*, a local quiz show in which contestants tried to guess the identity of silhouettes behind the screen. Eliot hosted that program, too. During the early 1960s, Channel 4 ran a series of daily one-hour specials for the two-week run of the Michigan State Fair. Eliot anchored those, too. And then there was *At the Zoo*, which ran from 1961 to 1979 and spawned two books plus a weekly newspaper column. *Eliot's Almanac*, a daily five-minute show featured Eliot talking about historical facts. And at one point, he even acted in a play with Johnny Ginger.

During the 1960s, Eliot's office at Channel 4 was a gathering place for celebrities, particularly sports figures. It wouldn't be unusual for him to meet up with the umpires and players from the evening's Detroit Tigers game at the Lindell AC, spending the night having fun and ending up at a schvitz until the wee hours. He knew everybody, from Detroit mayors and cultural chieftains to lawyers, judges and politicians.

In the end, what happened to Eliot happens to everybody in the medium, no matter how good they've been. He was fired at Channel 2 in 1982 during one of the station's purges.

After his stint at Channel 2, Eliot cobbled together yet another career. He handled weathercasting chores at WWJ-AM during the late afternoon and got voice-over work on commercials. He's a reminder of what broadcasting had been when it was unique and when it was something other than an ATM machine for another Wall Street company.

## Haynes, Trudy

Trudy Haynes desegregated Detroit television's news depart-ment. Said to be the first on-air African-American TV personali-ty in Detroit television news, she worked as a weathercaster at Channel 7 between 1963 and 1965. A graduate of Howard University, Haynes had broken into Detroit broadcasting as women's editor at WCHB-AM, where she hosted a daily program between 1956 and 1963.

Haynes was only on television for a short while, leaving Detroit in 1965 for Philadelphia's KYW-TV. Her stay there was consid-erably longer—33 years. Haynes desegregated Philadelphia, too, as the city's first African-American television reporter. While there, she interviewed everybody from President Lyndon B. Johnson and Martin Luther King Jr. to Tupac Shakur, according to her entry in the Broadcast Pioneers of Philadelphia Hall of Fame. She retired from KYW-TV in 1998.

Channel 7's Trudy Haynes desegregated Detroit television's news department.

## Hodak, Jerry

Hodak might be the most durable man in the history of Detroit television. His broadcast career spans nearly 40 years and two sta-tions: Channel 2 (1965-1977, 1992-1996) and Channel 7 (1977-1992, 1996-present). That's a longer, continuous on-air lifespan than George Pierrot, Bill Bonds, Sonny Eliot or any other Motor City video icon. All along, Hodak presented himself calmly, main-taining himself with admirable professionalism, doing his job with meticulous precision and noticeable lack of hype.

Hodak grew up on Detroit's east side, graduating from Denby High School. While attending Wayne State University, where he studied briefly under Dr. Everett R. Phelps, Hodak also worked at a $1-an-hour job at WABX-FM—a classical music station at the time. The job wasn't enough to keep Hodak afloat. As a result, he moved to Orlando, Florida, in 1961 to join his parents, who had recently emigrated from Detroit. That's where Hodak

Jerry Hodak: 40 years in television with-out losing his dignity.

Dr. Everett R. Phelps, "Mr. Weather."

first got into television, working at Orlando's CBS affiliate. He returned home to Detroit in 1965, and never left.

When Hodak started doing the weather, his work tools were maps and chalk. He now works with sophisticated Doppler weather radar equipment that can detect weather at literally any street corner. His command of meteorology and the physical sciences is said to be excellent, and his sober persona is refreshing in an increasingly loopy business.

### Phelps, Dr. Everett R. (d: 1961)

He was Channel 7's "Mr. Weather" in 1950, and Channel 2's meteorologist, 1951-1958. Phelps was more than a guy with a weather map, however. He had a Ph.D. in physics from the University of Michigan and co-wrote a textbook, *Practical Shop Mathematics*, which was translated into Italian. The book is considered a classic and is still used four decades after his death. In addition to Phelps' television appearances—some 2,000 during the 1950s—he had a day job since 1922 as a professor of physics and astronomy at Wayne State University.

Phelps prided himself on his background, which he said "enabled me to give a weather program in a manner which makes it more understandable to the average viewer." (Here was a man who wrote a Ph.D. dissertation: "The Fine Structure of the Near Infra-Red Absorption Bands of Water Vapor.") After the Soviet Union launched the Sputnik satellite in 1958, Phelps would explain to viewers when and where the spacecraft could be viewed. On the day after Christmas, figuring that Santa Claus had distributed new barometers to the area, Phelps would show viewers how to adjust the instruments to corrected sea level. He died at age 67, three years after leaving television.

### Shutty-MacGregor, Jo-Jo

Her infinite charm and unceasingly chipper attitude made her a

Jo-Jo Shutty-MacGregor, about to take flight in the CKLW-AM traffic chopper.

favorite on Channel 2 during the late 1970s and early 1980s. Several of the admiring biographies of Jo-Jo during the 1970s pointed out that she twirled a baton as a child. Nobody was surprised by the revelation.

A Detroit native and graduate of Michigan State University, Jo-Jo and her sister (who is now an anchorwoman in Chicago) would appear on *Milky's Party Time* and *Auntie Dee*. Fame would follow when she became the airborne traffic reporter on CKLW-AM. Although a flying traffic reporter is now a routine feature on drive-time radio, no station in Detroit had ever done this before CKLW News Director Byron MacGregor tried it. Jo-Jo, who had been working at Channel 4 in an off-screen capacity, was hired and launched above the rush-hour mayhem. She had a special chemistry with the other personalities on the air, and immediately became a Detroit celebrity. The chemistry with Byron MacGregor blossomed into an office romance and marriage in 1976.

When Channel 2 weathercaster Jerry Hodak jumped to Channel 7 in 1977, Jo-Jo got herself a weather gig. Her two-year tenure as the weatherperson included a few radical (for the time) departures. She often did the weather from remote locations outside of Channel 2's Southfield headquarters—from a cider mill, for instance, or from the bleacher seats at Tiger Stadium.

After leaving Channel 2, she worked in Flint throughout the '80s. Mostly recently, she could be heard statewide as the radio voice of the Auto Club of Michigan.

## Sillars, Mal

He was a meteorology teacher at Flint's Mott Community College when he started up a broadcast service for radio stations looking for ace weathermen. (His partner was John McMurray, who can still be heard on WJR-AM.) Sillars was more interested in the scientific end of weathercasting than the show-biz side. "I never cared much about television," he later said.

Channel 4's Mal Sillars.

That, of course, was exactly what Channel 4 was looking for during the early 1980s—Sonny Eliot's opposite, or at least somebody who wouldn't throw chalk at Mort Crim. Sillars became part of the Crim-Harlan-Smilovitz team that made Channel 4 very successful.

Later, Sillars was demoted to the morning newscast, leaving the station entirely. He now sells real estate in Buena Vista, Colorado, and says he has never been happier.

## Turner, Marilyn

Upbeat, pleasant, smooth, Marilyn Turner was the television embodiment of a woman with the world at her feet. She worked as the weathercaster on the evening news at Channel 2 and Channel 7. Each station held first place while she was there. Turner and husband, John Kelly, later hosted *Good Afternoon Detroit* and *Kelly & Company*, which enjoyed impressive ratings success during the 1970s and 1980s. As a model, she usually played—as she put it—"the neat, energetic homemaker, the trim young mother, or the cool, efficient airline stewardess." A close reading of *Good Morning, Detroit*, which is partly Turner's autobiography, reveals a focused, determined woman who fought for everything she ever got.

Turner (given name: Marilyn Miller) grew up in Windsor, Ontario. "From my earliest memories, I was always performing," she once wrote. She was Miss Hydro at the age of 4 and played accordion professionally while she was a child. She helped finance her husband, Bob, through med school. The marriage failed, was rekindled, but failed again. Turner was hired in as a "Miss Fairweather" at Channel 2, beginning a career as a weathercaster. This was at a time when women simply didn't work anywhere on a newscast, certainly not as an anchor or reporter.

It is no wonder that she lasted so long on the air, starting out as a weathercaster in the 1950s and remaining on the air until

Marilyn Turner: There at the beginning, there at the end.

*Company* went off the air in 1995. "I know now that I am fierce-ly independent. I don't like to have to ask anyone for permission to do anything." She was the kind of person who would have played well on a Vince Lombardi football team. Turner worked hard and was focused.

And she was there the day Detroit local television died. She'd hosted her show one Friday morning and was about to attend a lavish barbecue that had been laid out at Broadcast House. Station officials pulled the plug on the show, and her TV career.

# Backstage

*The most important work on television often goes on
in the executive suites and the editing rooms.
These people were influential in shaping Detroit television.*

## Alpert, Dan

He is Channel 56's heart, soul and institutional memory. Alpert joined Channel 56 in 1976 and rose to run its daily operations at the station, often serving as the station's public face. Earnest and sincere, he is a true believer in public TV's mission, which is to provide high-quality fare without regard to commercial potential. Since Alpert joined, three general managers have come and gone. But Alpert remains.

Alpert grew up in Chicago and graduated from Michigan State University, where he studied radio news. While there, he worked for WKAR-AM/FM, in addition to working two summers in New York City for *Radio Free Europe*. "It was like being in the center of the universe," he remembered. "My stories would be translated into Romanian, Bulgarian, Czech." After graduation, he joined WKAR-TV, Lansing's public television station. Alpert was hired initially as Channel 56's public information chief, and was appointed assistant general manager in 1982. His most recent promotion, in 2000, made him Detroit public television's chief operating officer.

## Antoniotti, Steve

He's in charge at Channel 56, Detroit's public television station. During the 1980s and into the 1990s, Channel 56 was noted for do-gooder programs such as *City For Youth*, which were designed to use the medium of television to improve life in Detroit. Under Antoniotti, the station moved away from that. It wasn't that Antoniotti thought that television should be used as a tool to make life worse. Antoniotti, instead, worked on moving Channel 56 into the big leagues of public broadcasting—on a par with public TV dynamos in Pittsburgh, Boston and elsewhere. For instance, the station joined with former NBC News correspondent Arthur Kent to produce *A Wedding In Basra*, a nationally broadcast documentary about everyday life in Iraq.

A Detroit native, Antoniotti (pronounced An-to-NET-tee) built an impressive resume in news and station management before joining Channel 56 in 1995. He learned TV production at Channel 4, moved to Channel 7 as a top producer, then moved on to New York's WABC-TV, Oklahoma City's KTVY-TV, Los Angeles' KNBC-TV and St. Louis' NBC affiliate. He joined Channel 2 in 1988, and presided over the station's raid of talent at Channel 7. The ratings didn't move appropriately, Antoniotti got sick of spending more time plotting profit margins than plotting actual TV programs, so he quit Channel 2 in 1995 and found a new home at Channel 56 later that year.

## Banks, William V. (d: 1985)

He founded Channel 62 in 1975, making it the first black-owned television station in the country. A lawyer, minister and broadcast executive by training, Banks' experience in broadcast-

William V. Banks founded the first African-American-owned TV station.

ing had been as president of WGPR-FM. Banks had also been a founding member of the International Free & Accepted Modern Masons, an African-American fraternal organization that was also one of the few African-American organizations that had a bank account big enough to help fund Banks' dream of building a Detroit TV station. The tab was $3 million, and the Masons peddled some of its real estate to pay the station's construction costs. After Banks scraped together commitments from advertisers for an equal amount, Channel 62 went on the air September 29, 1975.

The *New York Times* once described Banks as "a major figure in Detroit's black establishment." Banks described his dream to *Times* reporter William K. Stevens: "This (the founding of WGPR) means that blacks will be able to portray their civilization in the light of their interpretation of it. Heretofore, on television, it has been the way whites interpreted black civilization."

Banks' daughter, Tenecia Gregory, ran the station for several years. The Masons owned the station for some 20 years, before selling it to CBS Inc. for $25 million in 1995.

## Carino, Larry

He was Channel 2's head man between 1961 and 1975, and the station's community face throughout that period. Before Carino, most general managers stayed in their office, counting money and firing people. Carino was among the first to go in front of the camera to read editorials. He had many connections as a board member of Junior Achievement of Southeastern Michigan, Civic Searchlight and other organizations. He also sponsored the TV2 Swimmobile, a fleet of swimming pools on wheels that trekked to the town's poorer neighborhoods.

Under Carino, the news department grew from a tiny operation to an ambitious competitor that faded only after other stations raided Carino's newsroom. He also had something of a conservative streak, refusing to run an anti-war song, "The Big Muddy," on the Smothers Brothers television program in the midst of the Vietnam conflict.

## Clark, James F.

His tenure at Channel 4 (1953-1970) was the longest of any news director in the history of local television. One could argue that Clark was one of the most important figures in the development in TV news in Detroit. Under his leadership, Channel 4's news broadcasts usually had bigger audiences than Channels 2 and 7 combined. Not until the late 1960s, when Channel 2 put together the Jac Le Goff/John Kelly team, did another news operation present a challenge to Channel 4. That was almost a decade and a half into Clark's stewardship. Dick Westerkamp, Al Ackerman, Sonny Eliot, Ven Marshall, Kirk Knight, George Pruette and Dwayne X. Riley all worked for Clark. His influence was felt in radio, as well. Clark ran WWJ-AM's news department, one of the more aggressive operations in town. He shuffled his journalists between radio and television, giving them maximum exposure in two media. Clark ran both places with extraordinary ability and dedication.

A Detroit native and a graduate of Wayne State College (now Wayne State University), Clark started out as an announcer on WWJ-FM when FM was not considered important. After service in Europe during World War II, he returned to work as an announcer on WWJ-AM. In 1947, with Channel 4 putting the first TV signal into the local airwaves, Clark was there. He anchored the station's 6 p.m. and 11 p.m. newscasts. "It was more of a novelty at first," he later recalled. "Nobody could really comprehend the impact." He became the news department's leader in 1953.

Clark designed the "beat" system in Channel 4's newsroom. Before Clark, the custom had been to move reporters from one story to the next, almost at random. "They were like paratroop-

James F. Clark set the standard for Detroit's early TV news.

ers—they'd jump into a story and jump out," recalled Clark. Instead, Clark assigned reporters to single topics, so they could develop expertise—and thus report more intelligently. Kirk Knight, for instance, covered the Detroit Common Council. So when something happened at City Hall, Knight would know about it and discuss developments in some depth. Ven Marshall became an expert on the Teamsters and labor. Britt Temby reported on the United Auto Workers. "Unfortunately, television reporters had to be very, very shallow—jack of all trades—do a little bit of this, a little bit of that. It bugged me because they didn't research stories as they should be researched."

He also insisted that the reporters and anchors write their own scripts. "I was proud of our guys, because they not only developed their own stories, they had to do their own writing. As a result, they were very knowledgeable. ... I thought that what we did was put a little integrity in the television news business. I could see the way it was going—and it has developed into what I was afraid it was going to—a lack of integrity."

The result was that Channel 4's news—and the local TV news industry in general—was highly professional and geared more toward journalism than entertainment. And that may have been because Clark was in charge. "What he did was assemble the first credible local broadcast news operation in the country," said Bill Bonds, who tried without success to get Clark to hire him for his first TV job. Clark was not always an easy man to work for. But everybody gives the man high marks for integrity and honesty.

After 1970, he became Channel 4's editorial director, and became communications director for the Evening News Association in 1978, after the ENA swapped Channel 4 for Post-Newsweek Inc.'s station in Washington, D.C.

## Cunningham, Toby

Channel 50 Executive Producer Toby Cunningham may have

Toby Cunningham, Detroit's czar of live TV.

**Ron David witnessed the television medium during its infancy. He joined Channel 7 while still a student at Wayne State University, but quickly rose to the director's chair. David worked everywhere—"Lady of Charm," "Ed McKenzie's Saturday Dance Party," "Deadline: Detroit" and "Night Court." Forty years after leaving television for a successful advertising career, David still remembers the 1950s at Channel 7 as the most professionally satisfying years of his life.**

"Every day was an adventure. Everything was live. There was very little or no rehearsal of anything. At Channel 7, all of the directors and stage managers had five or six shows a day. We'd work all day doing television. After work, we'd go to the Alcove Bar, right next to the Maccabees Building (where Channel 7's studios were headquartered). It was a Damon Runyon bar. You had a combination of hookers, pimps and murderers all mixed in with the TV folks.

"We would try things. We'd do things like take a Dixie cup, paint the inside of it black and poke a hole in the bottom with a pencil. We'd put that paper cup over the lens and put somebody's head over a hole so we could superimpose the picture on the screen. That's how crude things were. Sometimes it worked. Sometimes it didn't. The fun part was that if you screwed up, everybody saw it.

"It was just a ball, one happy family. When I first started I was 17. I went to Wayne full time, and I was so eager to learn. All of the engineers there were really tough. I would beg them to let me run a camera. And they did. We would back each other up. It was fresh and new in those days. Nobody got paid a lot of money. As a matter of fact, I think I was making $50 a week; as a director, maybe $100-$200 a week. But we thought that was big money. The whole spirit of camaraderie was there, because we knew we needed each other badly, and we were trying to figure out this new animal called television.

"I sat down in a chair at 10:30 at night. I did a 15-minute weathercast back to back with 15 minutes with *Deadline Detroit*, back to back with *Soupy's On*, back to back with *Night Court*. I'd get out of the chair at 12:30 at night. And every single bit was live. We were young. We could take it. We loved what we were doing. We'd sign the station off, go to the Alcove Bar, drink until daylight, go home for a couple hours of sleep, and come back for more."

shaped more hours of live television than just about anybody in Detroit TV. Cunningham helmed Detroit Red Wings broadcasts between 1975 until 2003; produced Detroit Pistons basketball (1972-1979), Detroit Tigers baseball (1997-present) and Detroit Lions pre-season football (1992-1996, and again in 2004). Since sports has been Channel 50's specialty since it signed on in 1965, this makes Cunningham the most important producer in the station's history. In total, Cunningham estimates he produced more than 4,800 hours of live TV.

A native of Indianapolis, Cunningham was educated in Indiana University at Indianapolis, breaking into the television business as a stage manager and cameraman. He worked on Indiana Pacers basketball games, when the team was part of the American Basketball Association. Cunningham was hired at Channel 50 for the *Bill Kennedy* show in 1971. Come to think of it, producing a Bill Kennedy program might be great preparation for contact sport.

"(Cunningham) is unusual for television for being low-key and keeping his ego out of it. He's the calmest hand and steadiest influence I've ever seen," said Tom De Lisle. "His temperament is always the same—I saw him lose his cool only once." (It was a blow-up about an issue involving a TelePrompTer.) Cunningham was behind the hiring of Mickey Redmond, which turned out to be a masterstroke.

In addition to working at Channel 50, Cunningham has done freelance work for NBC Sports and ESPN. He did the Morgan State vs. Grambling football game at Yankee Stadium the day ESPN signed on the air in 1979.

## De Lisle, Tom

De Lisle, one of the most creative writer/producers in Detroit television starting in the 1980s, developed Count Scary and a Dick Purtan comedy special—both of which earned huge ratings for Channel 4. Later, he produced and wrote comic productions and sports—notably, some of the key portions of Channel 50's coverage of the last Detroit Tigers game at Tiger Stadium in 1999.

A Detroit native (De La Salle Collegiate High School and University of Detroit), De Lisle started his professional career as a copyboy at the *Detroit Free Press.* While still a student at the University of Detroit, he wrote for Dick Purtan. The Purtan parody song, "Pardon Me Roy, Is That the Cat Who Chewed Your New Shoes?" (sung to the tune of "Chattanooga Choo-Choo") is De Lisle's. Immediately after the 1967 Detroit riots, the *Freep* promoted him to reporter. De Lisle was a protégé of the late

James C. Dewey, a legendary *Free Press* rewrite man who was a key figure in the newspaper's 1968 Pulitzer for coverage of the social insurrection of the previous year. De Lisle left the newspaper in 1971 to work for Detroit Mayor Roman Gribbs.

After Gribbs left office, De Lisle spent the 1970s working in Hollywood as a comedy writer, where he penned gags for Richard Dawson (of *Hogan's Heroes* and *Family Feud* fame) and others, but he returned to his hometown in 1981 and joined Channel 4 as a producer. Within a year, he produced a Dick Purtan comedy special that earned World Series-type ratings. He was the writer on *Hamtramck*, which—controversial though it was—earned De Lisle an Emmy.

One of his best productions involved the closing moments of Channel 50's coverage of the last baseball game at Tiger Stadium. It featured a somber Al Kaline, alone in an empty stadium. Viewers saw Kaline step on home plate while Ray Lane read De Lisle's poem about the stadium's best days.

## Dempsey, Dr. John (d: 1982)

This Channel 2 news director and political analyst had successful careers in both government and academia after he left broadcasting. Dempsey joined WJBK-TV in 1956, the same year he obtained a Ph.D. in political science from the University of Michigan. He ran Channel 2's news department and/or worked as a commentator for a half-dozen years before going full time with the University of Michigan-Dearborn, where he taught until 1969.

Dempsey later worked for Governor William Milliken as state budget director (1973-1975), and director of the state's Department of Social Services (1975-1982). A heavy smoker, he died of lung cancer in 1982.

## Duffy, Mike

He has been the television czar at the *Detroit Free Press* for some two decades. As the top TV writer at the city's morning daily newspaper, he has more clout than just about anybody in print. *The Detroit News'* Frank Judge and the *Free Press'* Bettelou Peterson were serious and traditional. Duffy brought a sense of fun to the beat.

Duffy, an Ohio native and graduate of Denison University, was originally educated as a lawyer. He finished University of Iowa Law School, but decided against taking the bar exam—embarking on a newspaper career instead. His first job was at the *Port Huron Times-Herald,* where he worked as a weekend police reporter, education reporter, sportswriter and sports columnist. The *Freep* keyed in on his writing style and hired him as a feature writer in the mid-1970s. Within two years, he became the newspaper's TV writer—and one of the *Freep's* biggest names. With the exception of a two-year stint as a general columnist between 1988-1990, he's held the TV beat ever since.

## Findlater, Jeanne

She ran Channel 7 between 1979 and 1987, the year in which ABC Inc.—Channel 7's longtime owner—sold the station to Cincinnati-based Scripps Howard Inc. Her style was marked by the same magnificent charm, even when dealing with the town's biggest egos and worst buccaneers. Jeanne was very, very sweet. But you wouldn't want to mess with her. Bill Bonds credits her with saving his life.

Before TV, Findlater had something of a varied professional career. While in her early 30s, she taught developmentally disabled children in Detroit, and raised her two children on her own. The *Detroit Free Press* hired her as an editor of the newspaper's Sunday magazine during the 1960s, but she abandoned print in 1971 to become producer of Channel 7's *Town Meeting*. After a

Channel 7's Jeanne Findlater.

series of promotions, she became The Boss in 1979—the first female general manager of a major market television station. Her promotion says something about the iffy nature of power in television. Findlater was summoned to ABC's New York headquarters. She later told friends that she thought she was being fired. Instead, she got the keys to the building.

About Bonds and Findlater: When Bonds was hospitalized for depression, it was Findlater who helped him recover. During her reign, *Hot Fudge*—a classy children's show—was developed. Remarks one of Findlater's former charges: "These weren't the golden years. They were the platinum years." Between Findlater's style and ABC's free-spending ways, the place was great fun.

Employees at Channel 7 got a hint about what was to come when they saw how Scripps Howard officials got from Metro Airport to Broadcast House in Southfield. ABC officials would routinely show up in limousines. Scripps Howard officials got there in cabs. Findlater saw the future and quit the station not long after Scripps Howard bought the place in 1987. She now lives peacefully in Naples, Florida.

## Flynn, Bill (d: 2002)

Bill Flynn's rule at Channel 2 (1982-1987) was controversial. He fired people—Joe Glover, Beverly Payne and Sonny Eliot among them. Eliot's sacking caught people's attention.

Flynn had earned a reputation as a TV Mr. Fixit before he arrived in Detroit during the spring of 1982. Storer Broadcasting, Channel 2's owner, had assigned Flynn to the company's Boston station during the 1970s. It had no audience. Flynn captured the Boston-area broadcast rights to Boston Bruins hockey games, and the team won a Stanley Cup. Later, he went after the broadcast rights to the Boston Red Sox baseball team. The legend behind Flynn's Red Sox negotiation is classic: He visited the team's front office and tossed a $1 million check on the desk to get their attention. Flynn later cinched the deal, and the Red Sox won a pennant. Soon, everybody was watching the station. Flynn had performed a similar turnaround at Storer's Cleveland station.

There was no argument that Channel 2 needed fixing when Flynn got here. Sometimes, Channel 2's 6 p.m. newscasts had a smaller audience than *Buck Rogers* reruns on Channel 50. But his style made Flynn infamous. He canned Eliot moments before a newscast. "It's hard to come to work," Glover said at the time of his firing. "You develop the Sonny Eliot syndrome. You don't tie your tie until the last minute because you're not sure if you're going to be fired five minutes before you go on the air."

As unpopular as Flynn was at the time, some believe he was a visionary who knew which way the business was heading. Stations couldn't conduct business as usual any longer because the world was changing.

He once said in an interview, "I guess that was my mistake in saying the things I said about Sonny Eliot. But I don't take them back."

## Frank, Alan

He's Post-Newsweek's man at Channel 4. Not long after Post-Newsweek (publisher of both the *Washington Post* and *Newsweek* magazine) got Channel 4 from the Evening News Association in a swap for Post-Newsweek's Washington TV station, Frank was brought in as Channel 4's program manager. He was in on the ground floor of Channel 4's glitzy "Go 4 It" corporate image campaign and was promoted every few years. He became the station's programming chief in 1984 and general manager in 1991. By the year 2000, he was president of Post-Newsweek Stations Inc., but still lived in metro Detroit and had a major presence at the station's downtown Detroit studios.

A native of Pittsburgh, Frank served as a first lieutenant in the

U.S. Army during the Vietnam War. His television career began in earnest during the early 1970s, when he became production manager for the *David Frost Revue*. Later, he made stops at stations in Baltimore, Boston and San Francisco. He wasn't certain he'd stay long after arriving in Detroit in 1979, but he never left.

Under Frank, the station began broadcasting Detroit's Thanksgiving Day Parade and July 4th fireworks displays—both major TV events. While Frank was general manager, Channel 4's news department moved into a tough battle with Channel 7 for local TV news supremacy.

## Fyffe, Bill (d: 2000)

Fyffe was among the most influential newsmen, both in front of the camera and behind, during the early days of television. As an on-camera reporter at Channel 4, he was erudite and connected. When Channel 7 got serious about news in 1964, ABC hired Fyffe.

"He practically invented television news in Detroit," says Erik Smith, who worked for Fyffe. Among Fyffe's innovations here: He developed the use of "B roll" footage—showing video while an anchorman talked. "Until then, it was voice-overs and sound bites," says Smith.

He was one of the few managers in the history of Detroit local news who could tell Bill Bonds what to do. Fyffe ran the Channel 7 newsroom between 1964 and 1970. Later, he went on to become a general manager at Chicago's WLS-TV and New York's WABC-TV. He died after a fall while fixing a neighbor's roof in 2000.

## Graf, Richard (d: 1980)

He ran Channel 2's newsroom during the early and mid-1970s, and was one of the last "old time" newsmen to hold sway. Graf had worked at the *New York Times, The Denver*

Bill Fyffe put Channel 7 news on the map.

*Post,* and two now-defunct publications, the *New York Sun* and the *New York World Telegram.* Said one of Graf's protégés, Ron Sanders: "He quit more places because of principle than most people worked." He wasn't afraid to hire young people and was happy to infuse them with classic journalism values. Some of his hires included Sanders, Nancy MacCauley, Murray Feldman and Joe Glover.

Graf's pre-Detroit credentials included the news directorship at New York's WNBC-TV and news producer on NBC's *Today* show. He left Detroit for Boston's WNAC-TV and hired Ron Sanders to go with him.

He died at age 51 of heart disease.

### Griesdorn, Tom

He ran Channel 7 for about a decade, between the mid-1980s and mid-1990s. Those years, in general, were among the most tumultuous in broadcasting, especially at Channel 7. Griesdorn was faced with an increasingly competitive Channel 4, a downward-spiraling Bill Bonds and an ascendant cable television industry.

Griesdorn came to Broadcast House, Channel 7's Southfield headquarters, in 1982 as the station's controller. He was appointed general manager in 1987, a job he held until 1995. Griesdorn fired Bonds while Bonds was in an Atlanta rehab clinic. Bonds was notified by mail. Griesdorn left the station within the year, and now manages a TV station in Cleveland.

### Kapetansky, Seymour (d: 2001)

A Channel 4 writer and all-around utility man between 1951 and 1989, this Detroit native and Wayne State graduate started out in broadcasting in Hollywood, where he worked at ABC News and wrote for *Duffy's Tavern.* When pressing family business brought him back to Detroit, he stayed for good—first joining WXYZ-AM as a writer after World War II, then Channel 4 in 1951. He was Sonny Eliot's office mate—which explains how Kapetansky's name was often invoked in Eliot's routines. Kapetansky produced documentaries on Henry Ford and also hustled news of John DeLorean's acquittal in U.S. District Court on fraud charges onto the air before competitors could get there.

By the time of his retirement in 1989, he had grown into Channel 4's institutional memory—a rare and wonderful thing in a business that seems to have no memory of anything beyond last night's ratings book.

## Kell, Duane (d: 1996)

Kell ran Channel 50 from 1989 to 1996. He died in 1996 at age 49, after a long bout with cancer.

Under Kell's stewardship, Channel 50 made three significant moves: It kicked its 10 p.m. newscast into high gear, switched from the Fox network to the UPN network and landed local TV rights to Detroit Tigers baseball.

A Detroit native and a graduate of Wayne State University, Kell worked the sales side of the Detroit television business before joining Channel 50 in 1985 as director of sales and operations.

## Koste, Walt (d: 1998)

Koste was Detroit television's first, authentic television producer. At Channel 4, he developed *Playschool*, the *George Scotti Show* and *Let's See Willy Dooit*.

Before television, Koste worked as a radio actor and director, led a 14-piece dance band and wrote magazine stories. He joined WWJ radio in 1944, but switched to television when Channel 4 went on the air in 1947. Koste is considered among early television's most important figures.

Bob McBride asked: "Do you know where your children are?"

## McBride, Bob

If you made a list of "most important people at Channel 2," Bob McBride would rank near the top. At various points during his 21-year career there (1961-1982), with a hiatus as an anchorman in Chicago between 1971-1973, he was program manager, news director, station manager and general manager. He also read editorials. Detractors thought McBride oozed unctuousness; fans found him sincere.

McBride began his career as a copyboy at *US News & World Report*. He also worked in the *Detroit Free Press* promotion department before joining Channel 2 in 1961. He was promoted to news director, then elevated to general manager (the station's top job). One of his hires as news director was John Kelly, who went on to become one of Detroit's biggest on-air personalities.

It was his voice uttering the words "What do *you* think?"—the line that followed all editorials, thoughtful or not. McBride left Channel 2 in 1982 amid ratings trouble. The rest of his TV career was as a news anchorman in Washington, D.C., and Cleveland. McBride retired to Longboat Key, Florida.

## McCombs, Amy

She ran Channel 4 between 1981 and 1988, when the station solidified its position in Detroit. Plenty happened on her watch: The station opened a new building on West Lafayette, on the western edge of downtown Detroit; Channel 4's news division, led by Mort Crim and Carmen Harlan, took hold; and the station aired *Hamtramck*, for which McCombs apologized to the city's Polish community—an apology that was unnecessary, in the view of some observers.

A journalist by training, McCombs earned an M.A. from the Missouri School of Journalism, one of the best such schools in the country. General managers are mostly drawn from the sales ranks, making Post-Newsweek's appointment of McCombs in

1981 to the general manager's job somewhat unusual.

After leaving Channel 4 in 1988, McCombs went on to become general manager of Chronicle Broadcasting's KRON-TV, San Francisco's NBC affiliate. She also served as president of Chronicle Broadcasting, which included oversight of stations in Omaha and Wichita, plus oversight of BayTV, a 24-hour cable news and sports station in San Francisco. She retired from broadcasting in 2000.

## Meisner, Mort

Under Meisner's regime as Channel 2 news director during the 1990s, the station made a bold attempt to revitalize itself—mostly by raiding Channel 7. Meisner hired Rich Fisher, Jerry Hodak, Vince Wade, Catherine Leahan and Bill Bonds from Broadcast House. In the end, he had little to show for the raid: Although Hodak helped to successfully kick off Channel 2's early morning newscast, none of the Channel 7 crowd remained after Meisner was fired in 1997.

A Detroit native, Meisner studied broadcast journalism at the University of Detroit under Channel 7 News Director Phil Nye. He bugged Nye for a job, sitting outside Nye's office until Nye finally asked, in total exasperation: "If I give you a job, will you go away?" Meisner also worked in Chicago and St. Louis. He was asked to return to Detroit by Channel 2 General Manager Steve Antoniotti, an old friend from the Channel 7 days.

On paper, the Channel 7 raid should have worked. At one point, Meisner tried to lure Carmen Harlan from Channel 4 by offering her $500,000 a year for six years—an offer Harlan rejected. "What we didn't know—what nobody knew—was that raiding no longer works. It worked in the days when there were three stations, but it doesn't work when people have so many stations to choose from," Meisner later said. After Channel 2, he began a successful career as an agent.

## Nye, Phil

During Nye's watch as Channel 7's newsroom chief (1972-1974, 1976-1979), Channel 7 hired its biggest stars. Jac Le Goff, Diana Lewis, Marilyn Turner, Doris Biscoe, Jerry Hodak, John Kelly and Vince Wade were part of one of the most successful building efforts in local TV news history. Although Nye hired the talent with the aid of ABC's bountiful money supply, he got credit for forcefully melding the group into a credible, aggressive and unique news department.

Nye first came to town as a newsman for WKNR-AM, known to teenagers as "Keener 13." Although the station was famous for rock 'n' roll, WKNR's top managers felt that a strong news department would earn the station respect among advertisers. The station aired news at 15 minutes and 45 minutes after the hour, 24 hours a day. Nye, who was named the station's news director in 1964, demanded that each newscast be totally rewritten. Nye also produced annual news recaps each year between 1965 and 1969 on long-playing records. The station's 1967 news LP, which revisited the city's civil disturbance that year, remains a monumental piece of broadcast history. Nye is heard on the LP describing his experience crouched beneath a news vehicle as sniper bullets flew by. Consider the station's alumni list under Nye: Bill Bonds, Erik Smith, Vince Wade, Mike O'Neill and Ken Ford.

Nye spent time in Los Angeles between 1969 and 1972 as a newspaper editor and TV reporter/anchor before joining Channel 7 as news director in 1972. Those who worked for Nye always mention that he was tough and demanding. He cared about fairness, accuracy and use of language. "He was a Lou Grant type of newsman. And he didn't suffer fools gladly," recalls former Channel 7 reporter Vince Wade. With the front line of Bonds, Le Goff, Kelly, Turner and Ackerman, plus a stellar lineup of street reporters such as Jim Herrington, Vince Wade and Doris Biscoe, the station rose to No. 1 in the ratings. When two terrorists hijacked a commercial jetliner and threatened to crash it into a residential area of Detroit, Nye gave chase. He hired a Cessna and put a reporter aboard. When that wasn't fast enough, he rented a Lear Jet. This cost Channel 7 about $25,000. But Nye had the best coverage in town. As a reward for his work, Nye was transferred to New York's WABC in 1974.

He returned to Detroit in 1976 and stayed for three years before receiving two additional promotions in the ABC-owned station division. He was the head newsman for the five ABC-owned stations between 1979-1981, and station manager of San Francisco's KGO-TV from 1981 to 1984. He finished his career as part-owner of Burnham Broadcasting, which held stations in Green Bay, Bakersfield, Mobile and New Orleans. The group was sold to Fox Broadcasting in 1995. Nye produced a cooking show hosted by New Orleans chef Paul Prudhomme. He went into semi-retirement in Detroit in 2000.

## Ovshinsky, Harvey

He's the closest thing Detroit television has to an *auteur.* (That's a French word for somebody who makes really cool movies.) One of his television productions won a Peabody Award, the broadcast equivalent of a Pulitzer Prize. The rest of his work has won numerous Emmy Awards.

The son of inventor Stanford Ovshinsky, Harvey founded the *Fifth Estate*—Detroit's leading underground newspaper during the 1960s—just out of high school. Later, he joined WABX-FM as the station's news director. A few years later, he decided that television documentaries were his calling. During his career, he worked at Channels 4, 7 and 56. It probably says a lot about local TV that Ovshinsky can't get full-time work at any station. When he's not doing documentaries on his own, he also makes industrial films and teaches screenwriting.

Ovshinsky's work is original, unusual and very good—by anybody's standards. Most of his documentaries do not have a narrator. The subjects speak for themselves. And so does Ovshinsky's work.

## Peterson, Bettelou

She was the *Detroit Free Press* critic for some four decades before retiring in late 1993. Peterson began as a secretary at the *Freep* before introducing the newspaper's television column. Television was a curiosity to newspaper executives, and television critics weren't the high-profile writers they are now.

As the medium grew, so did Peterson's popularity—particularly since the *Detroit Free Press* circulation spiraled north from the 1950s on. It's easy to see why: She was the sole arbiter of video taste in Detroit's second-biggest newspaper, so her voice meant a lot. The *Detroit Free Press* later had as many as three reporters doing what Peterson did alone.

Her television question-and-answer column ran across the country. She'd answer questions such as: "What about Tatum O'Neal? I thought she was great in *Bad News Bears*. What other films has she done?" Or: "Whatever happened to Rosemary Clooney? Is she still in show business?"

## Pival, John (d: 1966)

He was the barely-in-control, drunken programming impresario who ran Channel 7 throughout its early years. Soupy Sales, Rita Bell, Bill Bonds, Dave Diles, Edythe Fern Melrose and Don Wattrick all owed their television careers to Pival. He could spot talent and inspire his charges. "If he told you a rooster could haul a locomotive, you'd hitch him up," says Dave Diles. On the negative side of the ledger: his boorish, violent behavior that would have gotten him fired instantly in the modern corporate environment.

A native east sider, Pival got into broadcasting after World War II. Pival had learned about video gear during the war. As the new medium of television developed after World War II, that knowledge made him the one-eyed man in the valley of the blind.

He had a knack for figuring what viewers wanted. He took chances. Nobody thought a golf tournament could be broadcast from a remote location, but Pival did. He hired a young comedian/dance show host named Soupy Hines and renamed him Soupy Sales, soon the hottest act in Detroit 1950s television. He found Dave Diles telling jokes at a celebrity roast. Pival discovered Rita Bell singing at a corporate outing.

Pival had a dark side, too. Former Channel 7 producer Ron David remembers a Christmas party in which Pival began picking on a producer. When the man talked back, Pival stripped to the waist and pummeled him. Dick Osgood's book, *W*Y*X*I*E Wonderland*, portrays a man who, in a drunken rage, chased a group of executives from his home with an axe.

The drinking and fighting with ABC's executives in New York ensured his exit from the station—but not before ABC wrote him an enormous check in gratitude. Pival drowned in Florida less than a year after his departure from Channel 7.

## Prato, Lou

Prato was Channel 4's top news executive between 1972 and 1975. Unfortunately for Prato, those were the years when nothing seemed to bounce Channel 4's way.

A Pittsburgh native, Prato arrived in Detroit in 1969 as an assistant to Channel 4 news director David Kelly. Channel 4's dominance of TV news, which it had enjoyed since television went on the air and flourished in the 1950s, had begun melting away. Channels 2 and 7 became stronger after the 1967 riots and nothing Channel 4 did throughout the 1970s seemed to make any difference.

Prato was an aggressive, scrappy newsman who wanted to make forays into investigative reporting. But Channel 4's owners vetoed some of the moves he wanted to make. And some of the station's on-air additions—such as hiring a Wayne

State University geography professor to critique NBC News each night—were forced on him. By the time Prato got the top news job, Channel 7 was cashing in on a brilliant rebuilding and promotional effort with the Bonds-Kelly-Ackerman-Turner team. Prato got to Channel 4 just in time to get hit by the steamroller.

After losing the news director's job in 1975, he went on to dual careers in academia and TV/radio news elsewhere. He taught at Wayne State University and Northwestern University's Medill School of Journalism, and Pennsylvania State University; worked as a news director in Chicago and Dayton; then settled in as a consultant in news writing, based in State College, Pennsylvania. His most fun accomplishment: writing a 670-page encyclopedia of Penn State football.

## Shurmur, E.L. (Hank) (d: 1970)

Channel 4's Hank Shurmur, a legendary early TV news cameraman, drank a lot and cussed a lot. He also was one of the most colorful characters in post-World War II journalism—one who instilled a sense of news values and innovation in TV's first generation of photographers.

Throughout the 1950s and 1960s, Channel 4 had no photographers of its own. Instead, the station hired Shurmur's company—NLU Productions. The initials stood for "Never Let 'Em Up," which accurately describes Shurmur's philosophy of news coverage. (So did the name of Shurmur's other company: Never Sleeps Newsreel Service.) Shurmur, in turn, hired his own people as subcontractors. As a result, his company processed every inch of film broadcast over Channel 4's airwaves well into the 1970s. Shurmur and *Detroit News* columnist Doc Greene were close friends, and terrorized downtown Detroit's saloons. He'd open many conversations with the phrase, "Lissen you sonofabitch..." as in "Lissen you sonofabitch, I had the best steak last night..." "He never meant anything by that," recalled Dwayne X. Riley, a Shurmur contemporary. "That was just the way he talked." Shurmur also created the "Ecclesiastical Shakedown Society," which raised tens of thousands of dollars for downtown Detroit's Holy Trinity Church. Nobody was immune from the Shurmur shakedown— including Bishop Fulton J. Sheen, who anted up $100 after getting the Shurmur treatment.

Before joining Channel 4, Shurmur worked as a public relations man and newsreel photographer, filming General George Patton's troops as they crossed the Rhine River during World War II. After the war, he had varying jobs, including handling bookings for bowler Andy Varipapa.

Everybody—from downtown Detroit bartenders to the presidents of the major auto companies—knew Shurmur. They'd show up at Shurmur's parties—dubbed "Slug Your Buddy" bashes because one could always count on a fistfight during the course of an evening. He was a friend of Teamsters President Jimmy Hoffa, who hired him to film Teamsters conventions. He once drank with President Harry Truman. Not long before he died, Shurmur's pals threw a party for him at Cobo Hall, probably the only place big enough to fit Shurmur's vast collection of acquaintances. Attendees included United Auto Workers President Walter Reuther, the current president of the United Auto Workers, two UAW-presidents-to-be (Leonard Woodcock and Doug Fraser); Detroit Mayor Roman S. Gribbs and a past mayor (Jerome P. Cavanagh). Also on the list of sponsors were a half-dozen judges and two congressmen. One of the speakers was New York Mayor Robert Wagner, a close friend of Shurmur's from World War II.

"Uneducated and obscene of speech, he never really realized what a good man he had become," the late Doc Greene wrote on the occasion of Shurmur's death. "Some of us did."

Hank Shurmur of the "We Never Sleep Newsreel Service."

## Snyder, Jim (d: 2001)

He was the first Post-Newsweek executive to hit town after Post-Newsweek Stations got Channel 4 in a swap with the Evening News Association. Among Snyder's hires: Mort Crim, Emery King, Mike Wendland and Jennifer Moore. He also made Carmen Harlan an anchor.

Snyder had been a Washington producer for CBS News before joining Post-Newsweek, which owns the *Washington Post* and *Newsweek* magazine, in 1968. While there, he hired Max Robinson, who went on to become an ABC News anchorman. Snyder arrived in Detroit in 1978, remaking the news department. He stumbled at first. Viewers may or may not recall reporters such as Victor Livingston. Snyder ended up firing 13 people in one day. But his plans for the station took root by the early 1980s—a thoughtful approach totally alien to the ambulance-chasing culture of these days. He placed a high premium on honesty, ethics and spirituality.

"To Snyder, it was a news director's job to know the community he worked in and what kind of newscast to put together," recalled Harrison S. Wyman, in an appreciation of Snyder's work after Snyder's death in 2001. "Snyder thought it was important that television news report stories you may not like to hear but needed to know." Said Terry Oprea, who worked for Snyder: "If there ever was a real-life Lou Grant, this was the guy. ... He really loathed the idea of covering murder for the sake of murder. He believed that if you were going to cover something like that, you had to have a reason. He wanted us to cover the culture, the fabric, the texture of the community." Heart problems forced Snyder's retirement from Channel 4, although he continued as a consultant to the company. He was replaced by his protégé, Bob Warfield.

## Stevens, Bob

Stevens' 44-year career as a Channel 4 cameraman (1955-1999) pretty much spans the growth of television news. He cov-

Even though he worked behind a camera, Bob Stevens always wore a coat and tie.

ered everything—murders, riots and Jimmy Hoffa's disappearance. Stevens combined the gruff style of a *Front Page* reporter with the sensitive eye of an artist.

A Detroit native and graduate of Cass Technical High School, Stevens knew early in life that he wanted to work behind a camera. "I decided when I was 11 that I wanted to be a photographer for *Life* magazine," he recalls. "When I went out on dates in high school, I almost always went to the Detroit Institute of Arts. I'd study the paintings."

Stevens worked as a photographer at Channel 9 during the early 1950s before joining H.L. Shurmur's We Never Sleep News Agency, which shot and developed all of the film for Channel 4 news. His work on a 1971 documentary about the Dodge mansion was especially noteworthy, and his thinking about lighting a scene featuring the Dodge dining room explains Stevens' eye. "I thought about it," he recalls, "and I asked myself, 'How would this place look if I came for dinner?'" Viewers saw a softly lit panorama, indeed, as if they were dining with Mrs. Dodge.

He had style, and was noted for two things: The first was his cigars. He smoked three or more a day for 25 years, until 1983. The second was his style of dress. Stevens always wore a coat and tie. "I never wanted people to think I was a bum," he said. On Stevens' last day at work, every television news photographer in Detroit—including the women—wore ties to work.

## Storer, George B. (d: 1975)

He developed Channel 2 into a Detroit TV force, and turned Storer Broadcasting Co. into one of the country's biggest TV station groups.

Storer came to Detroit during the late 1920s as a steel salesman. A detour into broadcasting was very successful: At one time he owned WJBK-AM, WXYZ-AM and Windsor's CKLW-AM, and also owned stations in Florida, Georgia, Ohio and West Virginia.

Newspaper readers learned about Storer's connections in high places during the late 1950s and early 1960s. A congressional subcommittee discovered that Federal Communications Commission Chairman John C. Doerfer had gotten around Miami and the Bahamas in Storer's private plane, and had hung around with Storer in Bimini. (Doerfer told the committee that he wanted to check out the signal from Storer's Miami station.) Later, a congressional subcommittee learned that Doerfer had been routinely entertained on Storer's yacht, the *Lazy Girl*, which was conveniently moored in Florida. All of this would have been business-as-usual, except that one of Storer's deejays had just been fired during a payola scandal.

Storer's empire was later sold to George Gillett, who sold it to Revson owner Ronald Perleman, who later sold it to Rupert Murdoch's Fox station group, which now owns the station.

## Strand, Pete

He was Channel 7's production chief during the 1950s, which made him Soupy Sales' boss. Strand, a New York native, joined Channel 7 in September 1948, a month before the station went on the air. Still in his 20s, Strand had something virtually nobody else had in the nation: television experience. He'd already worked at an experimental television station in New York City.

After arriving at Channel 7, Strand worked as a director on *Starlit Stairway*. He was appointed program manager in 1951. It was Strand, along with General Manager John Pival, who created *Lunch With Soupy*. After leaving Channel 7, Strand worked at WTTW-TV, Chicago's public television station.

## Talbert, Ted

He has produced more documentaries than anybody in Detroit about local African-American history and the African-American experience in the Motor City.

Talbert grew up in the Eight Mile/Wyoming neighborhood and graduated from Northern High School, where he was president of the Class of '61, a quarterback on the football team and second baseman on the baseball team. He later trundled off to the College of Southern Idaho, where he was the first black student, then to southern California, where he held a number of jobs.

Upon returning to Detroit in the 1960s, he worked as a standup comic before he got his first show: He helped produce *Haney's People*, and *Issues*, a show hosted by a young lawyer named Dennis Archer.

During the 1980s, Talbert began striking out on his own. He created some two dozen documentaries, all on local black history. Some of his topics have included the a history of black police officers in Detroit, a study of nurses in the military and a history of Detroit's black lawyers and judges. Talbert was inducted into the Michigan Journalism Hall of Fame in 2000. "Most of the people who made it into the Hall of Fame were either dead or over 60," Talbert said. "I was neither. I came in vertical."

## Upchurch, Al

Upchurch was Channel 7's news director at the start of the new millennium, but quit suddenly in mid-2000. A Michigan State University graduate, he started as a photographer in Huntington, West Virginia, before returning home to Detroit at Channel 7 in 1978. His first job at Channel 7 was as a writer on the weekend newscast. As the years went on, Upchurch took on more and more responsibility—becoming producer of the 5 p.m. and 11 p.m. newscasts and as executive producer in the news department. Upchurch served as second in command under a succession of three news directors—one of whom lasted only three weeks—before getting the top job in March 2000. He also won a half-dozen Emmy Awards.

He's one of a handful of news executives who was not intimidated by Bill Bonds and also has Bonds' respect. "I think they've got themselves the best news director in the country," Bonds said, upon hearing of Upchurch's appointment in March 2000. However, Bonds left his commentary post to do TV commercials for the Gardner-White furniture company shortly after Upchurch became news director.

## Warfield, Bob

Warfield ran Channel 4's news department during the 1980s, supervising the Mort Crim/Carmen Harlan pairing and laying the foundation for the station's news resurgence. Warfield attended Eastern Kentucky University, where he played basketball. He came to Detroit as assistant news director under Jim Snyder in 1979, shortly after Post-Newsweek bought Channel 4. Warfield moved to the top spot in the news department three years later, after Snyder was sidelined with a heart ailment.

Although Warfield left Channel 4 in the early 1990s, he didn't go far. He owns Alpha Capital Management, a financial management concern, which is located next to Channel 4's headquarters on West Lafayette in downtown Detroit.

## Weiss, Rube (d: 1996)

Weiss was the most beloved—and arguably among the most talented—of all of the figures in early local television. In front of the camera, he was Shoutin' Shorty Hogan on Soupy Sales' nighttime show. Weiss, an accomplished actor, also hosted Channel 7's *Tales of the Hawk*, in which he appeared on a South Seas-style set, unshaven and wearing a Hawaiian shirt. Off screen, he directed *Auntie Dee* and any number of popular shows.

Even before the television medium began in 1948, Weiss already had an extensive background both in radio and in the classroom. He had acted on numerous WXYZ-radio shows, including *The Lone Ranger, Green Hornet* and *Ned Jordan:*

Channel 7's Rube Weiss in a TV spot.

*Secret Agent.* Academically, he had earned a master's degree in English from what is now Wayne State University. He taught both English and drama at Detroit's Northern High School during the early 1950s.

Since virtually everything on local TV during the 1950s was live, directors were the dukes of the new medium. And Weiss was generally considered the wisest and kindest. "He had a heart of gold—one of the greatest people persons ever," recalled Ron David, a colleague from the station. "He'd help anybody at any time." After long days and nights of making television, Channel 7's staffers would retreat to the Alcove Bar, near Channel 7's studios in the Maccabees Building. "We were standing around one night and we looked around. In those days, everybody thought the big money would last forever, so everybody was blowing all of their money on the biggest cars, the fanciest clothes, etc.," recalled David. "Rube pointed this out one night and told me, 'Don't do that, Ron. Save your money.'" In the end, Weiss left the young medium with both his checkbook and dignity intact.

After leaving Channel 7, Weiss was much sought after as an actor and voice-over artist. Remember the radio ads "Sunday!!! Sunday at Motor City Dragway. Sibley at Dix"? That was Weiss. His voice is also heard on an educational tape of Henry James stories. Such was the man's range.

# *Acknowledgements*

I had a lot of help putting this book together.

Edward Peabody, Steven Wilke and Kelly Gehart of Momentum Books were wonderfully patient as this book came together. This book was originally developed and partially written for an earlier incarnation of Momentum, which was run by the late Ron Monchauk and the very-much-alive Bill Haney. Ron died as the project began, so there is no way of thanking him for his encouragement. Bill is alive and can be thanked. So thanks, Bill.

Ed Golick was of great assistance. He has a passion, love and scholarly interest in popular culture, and helped fill in the gaps of this book. His Web site, www.detroitkidshow.com, is great fun; the late Mark "Doc" Andrews, who had a flawless memory and sharp intellect, was of great assistance; Ron David was particularly helpful about television in the 1950s, and was nice enough to share with me the personal, unpublished memoirs of his father, Toby David. Deborah Gordon was generous in her time as she shared tapes of her father, Lou Gordon. She also helped me understand what Gordon meant to journalism in this town. Channel 7's Marla Drutz—In my opinion, a shining example of broadcast integrity—also aided the project.

This project would have been impossible without the *The Detroit News* library staff, which was unfailingly generous with their time when I worked there between 1987 and 2002. That would include Vivian Baulch, Linda Culpepper, Kay Houston, Anita Mack, Laurie Marzejka, Zena Simmons and Pat Zacharias. Bridgit Baulch helped me dredge up several wheelbarrows full of clips. I had a blast working at the *News,* and would like to thank everybody there.

David Poremba and Susan Kelly at the Burton Historical Collection were wonderful. So was William LeFevre, at the Walter P. Reuther Library of Labor and Urban Affairs; and Patience Nanta at the Detroit Historical Museum.

Lately, I've been doing occasional work for the *Detroit Free Press,* where Steve Grimmer and Steve Byrne have been especially kind to me. I also worked there between 1970 and 1987, and was lucky enough to work for Kurt Luedtke and Neal Shine. Both men have been astonishingly helpful to me throughout my life.

Thanks to Paul and Anita Lienert, Bob Giles and Bob Stevens. Special thanks to the *Detroit Free Press* library staff of Ruth Miles, Chris Kucharski, Barb Loth, Shelley Lavey and Patrice Williams. Also thanks to all of my friends at WWJ-AM, but especially Rich Homberg, Georgeann Herbert and Pam Woodley.

Toby Cunningham, Patricia Mills, Phil Nye, Dwayne X. Riley, Kathleen Ryan, Joe Lapointe, Bill McGraw, Dave Diles, Tony Stevenson, Paul Prange, Gail Pebbles, Aileen Bower, Jim Chylinski and Patricia Kukula Chylinski, Tom Greenwood and James F. Clark all provided support. The folks at John K. King Books in downtown Detroit were cheerful friends throughout the project. So thanks to Thomas R. Schlientz, John K. King, Marley King and Deborah Lee.

And thanks to Lee Alan, John Fairley, Bill Bonds, Poonam Arora, Tom De Lisle, Elaine Dietz, Terri Turpin-Amato, Joe Berwanger, Audrey Fish, Carolyn Kraus, Ken Hissong, Hal Sullivan, the late Seymour Kapetansky, Henry Maldonado, Christine Zampa, and Mary and Pete Casinelli for generously sharing their time and memories with me. A huge thanks to Dr. Mel Small, my history teacher at Wayne State University, who has been patient with me, and encouraged me to research and think deeper. And the biggest thanks of all goes to Sonny Eliot, who put up with daily telephone calls from the author seeking obscure information.

# *Author Bio*

Tim Kiska covered the television industry for *The Detroit News* between 1990 and 2002. A native Detroiter, he worked at the *Detroit Free Press* between 1970 and 1987, where he covered courts, the automotive industry and held various other reporting assignments. He joined *The Detroit News* in 1987. Kiska completed work on a Ph.D. in history at Wayne State University in 2003 and currently teaches journalism at the University of Michigan-Dearborn.

Tim Kiska consulted with his muse, White Fang, when writing this book.

Photo by: Kathleen Ryan

# Photo Credits

**Key:** photo subject; courtesy of

## Chapter 1
(Page 4, clockwise)
Clyde Adler; Jane Adler
Milky the Clown; Peggy Tibbits
Sgt. Sacto; Tom Ryan
Ricky the Clown; Ed Golick
Captain Jolly; Ron David
Soupy Sales; WXYZ
The Faygo Kid; Faygo Beverages Inc.
Poopdeck Paul; Matt Keelan
Detroit kid show hosts; Peggy Tibbits
Jingles; Matt Keelan
(center) Bozo; Art Cervi

(Pages 5-23)
Clyde Adler; Jane Adler
Bozo; Art Cervi
The Faygo Kid; Faygo Beverages Inc.
Jingles; Matt Keelan
Miss Flora; Ed Golick
Johnny Ginger, Sammy Davis; Johnny Ginger
Hot Fudge Gang; Bob Elnicky
Bwana Don and Bongo Bailey; Ed Golick
Captain Jolly; Ron David
Milky and Creamy; Peggy Tibbits
Milky the Clown; Peggy Tibbits
Oopsy, Bob Elnicky; Bob Elnicky
Poopdeck Paul; Matt Keelan
Ricky the Clown; Ed Golick
Sgt. Sacto; Tom Ryan
Soupy Sales; WXYZ
Soupy Sales, White Fang; Jane Adler
Larry Sands; Lori Wagner
Herkimer Dragon, Cecil B. Rabbit; Matt Keelan
Sagebrush Shorty; Ed Golick

## Chapter 2
(Page 24, clockwise)
Mort Neff; WXYZ
Bill Kennedy; WKBD
Jerry Chiapetta; WXYZ
Dennis Wholey; WTVS
Bob Hynes; WXYZ
George Pierrot; Burton Historical Collection
Edythe Fern Melrose; Carol Bainbridge
Mr. Belvedere; Maurice Lezell
Rita Bell; WXYZ
Mary Morgan; Matt Keelan
(center) Conrad Patrick; Matt Keelan

(Pages 25-63)
Ed Allen; Sonny Eliot
Bob Allison; Sonny Eliot
Sonny Eliot; Sonny Eliot
J.D. Beemer; Carol Bainbridge
Rita Bell; WXYZ
Chuck Bergeson; Ed Golick
Bob Hynes; WXYZ
Jerry Chiappetta; WXYZ
Mr. Belvedere; Maurice Lezell
Bill Kennedy; Ed Golick
Bill Kennedy; WKBD
J.P. McCarthy; WKBD

Cathie Mann; Sonny Eliot
Bob Maxwell; Marilyn Bond
Edythe Fern Melrose; Carol Bainbridge
Fred Merle; Fred Merle
Mary Morgan; Matt Keelan
Mort Neff; WXYZ
Conrad Patrick; Matt Keelan
George Pierrot; Burton Historical Collection
Gil Maddox; Sue Marx
Johnny Slagle; *Detroit Free Press*
Pat Tobin, Johnny Slagle; Ed Golick
John D. Watts; *Detroit Free Press*
Dennis Wholey; WTVS
Fred Wolf; Ed Golick

## Chapter 3
(Page 64, clockwise)
Sir Graves Ghastly; WJBK
Morgus; WJBK
Count Scary; Tom Ryan
The Ghoul; Ron Sweed

(Pages 65-69)
Sir Graves Ghastly; WJBK
The Ghoul; Ron Sweed
Morgus; WJBK
Count Scary; Tom Ryan

## Chapter 4
(Page 70, clockwise)
The Sheik; Arena Publishing
Bull Curry; Arena Publishing
Fritz Von Erich; Arena Publishing
Johnny Valentine; Arena Publishing
Bobo Brazil; Arena Publishing
Bull Curry; Arena Publishing
Ernie Ladd; Arena Publishing
The Sheik; Arena Publishing
(center) Dick the Bruiser; Arena Publishing

(Pages 71-79)
Bobo Brazil; Arena Publishing
Dick the Bruiser; Arena Publishing
Leaping Larry Chene; Arena Publishing
Bull Curry; Arena Publishing
Ernie Ladd; Arena Publishing
Lord Layton; Arena Publishing
The Sheik, Abdullah Farouk; Arena Publishing
The Sheik; Arena Publishing
Johnny Valentine; Arena Publishing
Fritz Von Erich; Arena Publishing

## Chapter 5
(Page 80, clockwise)
Nat Morris; Nat Morris
Stan Wisniach, Harry Jarkey, Jimmie Stevenson, Irv Romig; Carol Bainbridge
Joel Sebastian; Marilyn Bond
Nat Morris with dancers; Nat Morris
Ed McKenzie, George Young; Marilyn Bond
Jack Surrell; Marilyn Bond
Robin Seymour; Marilyn Bond
(center) Bud Davies; Matt Keelan

(Pages 81-87)
Lee Alan, Pixies Three, Joel Sebastian; Marilyn Bond and Lee Alan

Stan Wisniach; Carol Bainbridge
Bud Davies; Matt Keelan
Ed McKenzie, George Young;  Marilyn Bond
Ed McKenzie; Ed Golick
Dee Parker; WXYZ
Nat Morris with dancers; Nat Morris
Nat Morris; Nat Morris
Robin Seymour; Marilyn Bond
Jack Surrell; Marilyn Bond

## Chapter 6
(Page 88, clockwise)
Doris Biscoe; WXYZ
Vince Wade; WXYZ
Dwayne X. Riley; Dwayne X. Riley
Lou Gordon; WKBD
Reporter crowd scene; Bob Stevens
Bill Bonds; WXYZ
Bob Bennett; Bob Stevens
Robbie Timmons; Sonny Eliot
WWJ Newsroom; WDIV
Carmen Harlan, Mort Crim;WDIV

(Pages 90-147)
Bob Bennett; Bob Stevens
Doris Biscoe; WXYZ
Jerry Blocker; Jerry Blocker family
Bill Bonds; Ed Golick
Bill Bonds; WXYZ
Vic Caputo; Sonny Eliot
Carl Cederberg; *Detroit Free Press*
Carmen Harlan, Mort Crim; WDIV
Neal Shine; WTVS
Joe Glover; WKBD
Lou Gordon; WKBD
Austin Grant; Matt Keelan
Hubert Humphrey, Don Haney; Don Haney
Jim Herrington; WXYZ
John Kelly; Sonny Eliot
Kirk Knight; WDIV
Jac LeGoff; Sonny Eliot
Davey Marlin-Jones; Ed Golick
Byron MacGregor; Jo-Jo Shutty-MacGregor
S.L.A. Marshall; Texas Tech University
Ven Marshall; WDIV
Dean Miller; Ed Golick
Terry Murphy; *Detroit Free Press*
Guy Nunn; *Detroit Free Press*
Beverly Payne; Sonny Eliot
Dwayne X. Riley; Dwayne X. Riley
Ron Sanders; Sonny Eliot
Wes Sarginson; Sonny Eliot
Jerry Stanecki; Sonny Eliot
Ken Thomas; WKBD
Robbie Timmons; Sonny Eliot
Vince Wade; WXYZ
Dick Westerkamp; WDIV
Paul Williams; WDIV

## Chapter 7
(Page 148, clockwise)
Al Ackerman; Sonny Eliot
Ty Tyson; WDIV
Van Patrick; Detroit Lions
Dizzy Trout; Ed Golick
Ray Lane; WKBD
Vince Doyle, Anne Doyle; Anne Doyle

Budd Lynch; *Detroit Free Press*
Ernie Harwell; *Detroit Free Press*
(Pages 149-173)
Al Ackerman; Sonny Eliot
Dave Diles; WXYZ
Anne Doyle; Anne Doyle
Ernie Harwell; *Detroit Free Press*
Don Kremer; Don Kremer
Ray Lane; WKBD
Budd Lynch; *Detroit Free Press*
Van Patrick; Detroit Lions
Dizzy Trout; Detroit Public Library
Ty Tyson; WDIV
Don Wattrick; *Detroit Free Press*

## Chapter 8
(Page 174, clockwise)
Sonny Eliot, Annette Eliot; Sonny Eliot
Jerry Hodak; WXYZ
Dr. Everett Phelps; *Detroit Free Press*
Sonny Eliot; Sonny Eliot
Jo-Jo Shutty-MacGregor; Jo-Jo Shutty-MacGregor
Marilyn Turner; Sonny Eliot
Trudy Haynes; Trudy Haynes
Mal Sillars; Mal Sillars

(Pages 175-181)
Sonny Eliot; Sonny Eliot
Sonny Eliot, Annette Eliot; Sonny Eliot
Trudy Haynes; Trudy Haynes
Jerry Hodak; WXYZ
Dr. Everett Phelps;
Jo-Jo Shutty-MacGregor; Jo-Jo Shutty-MacGregor
Mal Sillars; Mal Sillars
Marilyn Turner; Sonny Eliot

## Chapter 9
(Page 184, clockwise)
Toby Cunningham; WKBD
Hank Shurmur, Bob Stevens, Bill Flemming; Bob Stevens
Bob Stevens; Bob Stevens
BobMcBride; Sonny Eliot
Bob Stevens; Bob Stevens
Rube Weiss; Leon Weiss
James. F. Clark; WDIV
Bill Fyffe; WDIV
Hank Shurmur; WDIV
Jeanne Findlater; WXYZ
(center) William Banks; Nat Morris

(Pages 186-212)
William Banks; Nat Morris
James F. Clark; WDIV
Toby Cunningham; WKBD
Jeanne Findlater; WXYZ
Bill Fyffe; WDIV
Bob McBride; Sonny Eliot
Hank Shurmur; WDIV
Bob Stevens: Bob Stevens
Rube Weiss; Leon Weiss